INTRODUCTION TO
Mexican American Studies

CUSTOMIZED VERSION OF
"INTRODUCTION TO MEXICAN AMERICAN STUDIES:
STORY OF AZTLAN AND LA RAZA"
2ND EDITION BY ARTURO AMARO-AGUILAR

MI GENTE

FRANK PADILLA PH.D.

Kendall Hunt
publishing company

Dedication

Thanks to their support and *cariño*,
this work is dedicated to
my wife Dolores
and family
Alex,
Maricela, Sid, Marcos,
Sylvia,
and
Ariana Amaro

CONTENTS

CHAPTER 5   The Early and Late 1800s: Life and Culture of Mexicans before and after the War   57

CHAPTER 6   The Early 1900s: The Trials and Tribulations of Social and Cultural Change   65

ACKNOWLEDGMENTS

I would like to give a sincere thanks to the contributors to this work. You have made a very valuable contribution to our students in Chicano-Latino Studies. A sincerely felt thanks to my professors and colleagues. A special thanks to Professor Matt Espinoza Watson, J.D., for his critical thinking and suggestions. Professor Matt Espinoza Watson is a very creative scholar and community activist. Maybe most importantly, I need to acknowledge my many students over the years. I am indebted to them for their quest for knowledge. Their critical questions provided much valuable insight. *Gracias.*

CHAPTER 1

INTRODUCTION

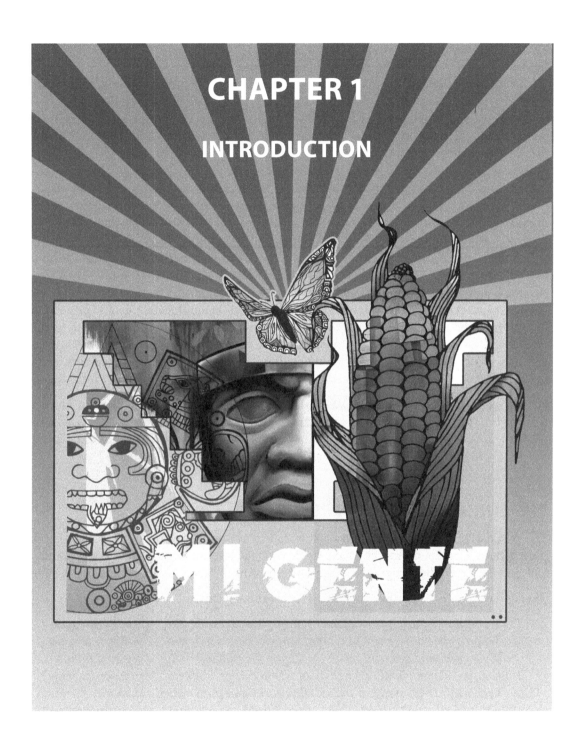

This book is the story of Mexican Americans. It is a general survey and interweaves the cultural and historical roots of *La Raza* going back thousands of years.

The academic field of study is known as Mexican American Studies. On some college campuses, it may be known as Chicano-Latino Studies. These programs focus on the history, heritage, and culture of Mexican Americans and other Latinos in the United States. An overlapping, related academic program is Latin American Studies. Programs in Latin American Studies focus on the history, heritage, and culture of the many countries of *Latino América,* including the Spanish-speaking Caribbean countries, *El Caribe.* Some universities may also have specific programs in Caribbean Studies that include the rich cultural diversity of the entire region. Occasionally, colleges and universities incorporate related studies under the heading of Ethnic Studies or Cultural Studies. These colleges may use this option in order to administratively align the various studies of ethnicity and culture under one rubric or category.

Ethnic Studies programs generally include various subprograms, such as Chicano-Latino Studies, Native American Indian Studies, African American Studies, and Asian American Studies. These courses span social sciences, humanities, and the arts. It may be well advised for students to major in Ethnic Studies, especially as they look at jobs and professions in relation to cultural diversity in the United States and the global and international dynamics of economics and politics. Ethnic Studies are popular undergraduate majors. The curriculum provides students with a strong academic foundation for those planning careers in law, health, education, social work, business, industry, and government civil service professions.

Note to Students   Go to http://www.ethnicstudies.org to learn about the National Association for Ethnic Studies (NAES), an association of ethnic studies professionals in academia. See http://www.ethnicstudies.ucr.edu for an example of a university that offers a doctorate in ethnic studies.

THE CHICANO-LATINO PERSPECTIVE

The purpose of this book is to expose the student reader to a variety of Chicano-Latino perspectives. These perspectives have evolved over the last few decades with the creation of Chicano-Latino Studies programs throughout the country in many colleges and universities.

The following statement reflects the overall goals and objectives:

> *The mission and purpose of Chicano-Latino Studies includes: (1) Ensure a comprehensive program with a curriculum that provides both depth and breadth by offering a broad range of solid academic courses; (2) provide students with the best and finest of academic scholarship and research available to college students; (3) prepare students for further advanced study in the social sciences and humanities; (4) with the study of Chicano-Latino history, heritage, and culture, provide students with an awareness and knowledge of the fastest growing identifiable ethnic cultural population and their*

role and contribution to American society. The Chicano-Latino Studies program is a viable program offering an interdisciplinary and multidisciplinary curriculum. Chicano-Latino Studies advances the mission, goals, and objectives of the college in terms of a program that is reflective and meets the academic and educational needs of the rich cultural diversity of American society.

Chicano-Latino Studies programs have become a strong and viable academic discipline since they were established in the late 1960s. Community people and activists, recognizing the educational needs of the community, were especially pivotal in implementing the programs. The proliferation of Chicano Studies was the direct result of the *Chicano Movement*. The movement, *el movimiento,* was a civil rights/human rights/cultural rights struggle to promote social and cultural change. In the educational sphere, Chicanos and Chicanas worked tirelessly to make schools, colleges, and universities sensitive and receptive to the educational needs of the community. Colleges and universities throughout the United States now offer classes in Chicano-Latino Studies. Programs in this major range from associate degrees to Ph.D.s. The many classes offered depend on the emphasis of each program and the academic expertise of the faculty.

<u>Note to Students</u>   For an example program, go to http://www.chicst.ucsb.edu to learn more. The University of California—Santa Barbara offers bachelor's, master's, and doctorates in Chicana and Chicano Studies. Go to http://www.naccs.org to learn about the National Association for Chicana and Chicano Studies (NACCS), an association of professionals in academia that allows student membership.

DEFINITION OF TERMS: THE USE OF ETHNIC AND RACIAL TERMS AND LABELS

Every field of study has words or vocabulary used in a specific way with a given meaning. Notice that the same word may be defined differently in various fields of study. Take, for example, the word *assimilation*. The concept of assimilation may be used one way in biology, a different way in psychology, and still another in anthropology. So it is with Chicano-Latino Studies. Vocabulary words specific to our field of study have developed a particular meaning. From a Chicano-Latino Studies perspective, what does it mean when we say that Mexican Americans become assimilated? This assimilation process will be discussed in subsequent chapters. (See the Glossary for the definition of assimilation as used in Chicano-Latino Studies.)

Of special interest are the many ethnic and racial terms and labels used in American society. Consider the influence of the mass media. *Mass media* are the vehicles of mass communication, including newspapers, magazines, television, radio, and the Internet. How do the mass media identify Latinos? This poses complex social and cultural issues. Confusion, conflict, or disagreement may exist not only in society but also among Latinos themselves in relation to the use of ethnic identifiers. From a Chicano-Latino perspective, the most critical issue of cultural survival is that Latinos must define their own cultural identity, reality, and existence.

Ethnicity and race play a prominent role in American society today. Issues related to race and ethnicity—including immigration, trade, and government—are common on the daily news at home and across the world. Stories related to events across or within the U.S. border sometimes refer to Mexicans, sometimes to Hispanics, sometimes to Latinos. But how do Latinos respond to the question, "What do you prefer to call yourself?" Who is Mexican? Who is Mexican American? Who is Chicano or Chicana? Who is Latino or Latina? Who is Hispanic? Who is Spanish? We need to be clear to avoid confusion; therefore, it behooves us to define the use of ethnic and racial terms and labels. Here are some key terms and explanations:

Mexican. Strictly defined, a Mexican is a person born in México. Of the more than 51 million Latinos in the United States today, many were born in México. Similarly, there are many Latinos born in Chile, Colombia, El Salvador, Guatemala, Nicaragua, and every country of Latino América and the Spanish-speaking countries of the Caribbean, El Caribe. Frequently, the U.S. mass media will use the term Mexican national, referring to a person born in México, and technically this is correct.

Mexican American. This refers to an American of Mexican descent. Frequently, the parents, grandparents, or other relatives were born in México. The Mexican American is a citizen of the United States. However, rather than uttering the lengthy *Mexican — American,* many feel comfortable simply identifying as *Mexican.* Mexican Americans often state, "Why should I say American when it is obvious that I was born and live in the United States?" Many Mexican Americans identify and relate with the cultural roots of their family from the old country. The use of the term *Mexican* can be a comfortable fit for Mexican Americans today. Individuals not aware of the Latino culture and community might ask, "Why do you call yourself Mexican? You are American because you were born in the United States!" A Mexican American might respond, "I call myself *Mexican* because I am proud of the history, heritage, and culture of my parents, grandparents, and relatives from México! It's a matter of cultural identity, pride, dignity, honor, and respect!"

Chicano and Chicana. These terms were greatly popularized with the Chicano Movement of the 1960s and 1970s. Chicanos and Chicanas were Mexican Americans who started a social movement within the community. The movement was a struggle for civil rights, human rights, social justice, and equality. It also included a cultural revolution and cultural renaissance. These will be topics of much discussion in future chapters, especially Chapter 7.

Latino and Latina. There are more than 52 million Latinos-Latinas in the United States today. *Latino-Latina* is an umbrella term referring to people in the United States with cultural roots in México and the many countries of *Latino América* and the Spanish-speaking countries of *El Caribe.* The vast majority of Latinos in the United States are of Mexican descent.

Hispanic. Like the use of the label Latino, *Hispanic* is an umbrella term meaning people of Spanish-speaking origin. *Hispanic* is frequently used by government institutions and the mass media in American society. Based on the Chicano-Latino perspective, the term *Hispanic* will not be recommended nor used in this book due to social, cultural, and political reasons that will be clarified in due time. The *Hispanic* label historically emphasizes the white Spanish European history, heritage, and culture. By definition, the Hispanic label deemphasizes the rich Indian indigenous cultural roots of Latino culture.

Spanish. The Spanish are in Spain. In the United States, people identifying as Spanish have parents and relatives whose cultural root is Spain. Spain means Spanish culture and civilization. Spain imported and imposed the Spanish language and culture into the Américas with the Spanish conquest. Due to this, the Spanish language is a huge part of Latino culture. It is always humorous to hear someone say, "Do you speak Mexican?" Mexican is a cultural group, not a language!

La Raza. *La Raza* literally means "the race" or "the people," referring to Latinos in the Américas. In a sense, it is a term of endearment manifesting affection for the people and the culture. It is commonly used in the phrase *Viva la Raza,* meaning "Long live the people," or "Long live the race." The concept of *La Raza* has a multiplicity of historical and cultural dimensions explained in future chapters.

Note to Students   See Glossary: Mestizo, Mezcla, Mestizaje.

Other ethnic and racial labels and terms will be defined in their appropriate time as our chronological study follows thousands of years of cultural roots. To understand Mexican Americans is to understand the dynamic influence and impact of history, heritage, and culture. These ethnic labels are not merely casual terms. Instead, it is important to understand the deep, underlying cultural meaning. To some people, the terms may be provocative and explosive. Words command power and may be used to unite or divide. Cultural identity is at the heart of one's personal identity. Subsequently, when Latinos-Latinas say *mi gente,* my people, it is a source of cultural identity and cultural pride.

Note to Students   The purpose of this book is to expose the reader to a variety of perspectives. From the academic point of view, we will use the paradigm of *Chicano-Latino perspective.*

Note to Students   It must be made clear that the *Chicano–Chicana perspective* is rooted directly in the Chicano Movement of the 1960s and 1970s. The *Latino–Latina* perspective is more varied and difficult to clearly define. They have much in common through language and culture. Yet, Latinos–Latinas are multiethnic, multiracial, and multicultural. The Latino community throughout the United States is a very diverse population. Diversity can be seen in the social and cultural differences between the various Latino communities. It is the student's task to compare and contrast the social and cultural similarities and differences between the Latino groups. For example, *Mexicanos, Puertorriqueños, Cubanos,* and *Dominicanos* have their own unique and distinct cultures.

THE CONCEPT OF CULTURE: CULTURE IS DYNAMIC

What is culture? What are cultural values and beliefs? What is cultural behavior? Culture is a critical concept to understand. Culture is a configuration of customs, traditions, rituals, and celebrations. Common examples include arts, crafts, music, dance, theater, literature, folklore, foods, and cooking. These cultural elements are unique and distinct to a group of people. This group is called a cultural group with a distinct cultural identity. People within a cultural group identify with one another and with their history, heritage, and culture.

Learned Culture

Individuals internalize culture through their socialization. Socialization is a process whereby the individual internalizes the values, beliefs, and behaviors of his or her family, culture, community and society. The individual is therefore a product of his or her social and cultural environment. Growing up, the person learns to think, believe, and act in accordance with the cultural group that provided the socialization. Generally, the individual displays values, beliefs, attitudes, and behaviors that are within the parameters of the cultural group. A prime example is the socialization that occurs within the family. The family is a basic social institution in American society. From the perspective of society, a major function of the family is the socialization process of the child. This ensures that the culture is transmitted to successive generations.

One's culture defines cultural norms or standards of behavior. However, the individual has the personal option to pick and choose. What are examples of Mexican Americans internalizing Mexican culture? What do you think of Mexican Americans who enjoy Mexican folkloric dancing and listening to Mexican music? In contrast, individuals may decide to deviate and defy cultural norms. What are examples of Mexican Americans who make the personal choice not to adhere to Mexican culture? What do you think of Mexican Americans who do not identify with Mexican culture and instead wish to assimilate into the mainstream of American society? What occurs in a family situation when a Mexican American decides to marry someone not Mexican? In the final analysis, the individual navigates through an ocean of many cultural options and alternatives.

Created Culture

Individuals, family, community, and society create culture. On one hand, culture is inherited from previous generations, and on the other hand, people create their own version and rendition of culture to fit their own needs at the time. Remember that cultural change is always part of the equation. Culture appears to remain constant and continuous, but culture is also changing continuously. Society requires a degree of cultural continuity from generation to generation.

Traditional Culture

In understanding the dynamics of culture, a description of traditional culture is a convenient starting point. We say that people adhering to traditional culture have traditional values, beliefs, attitudes, and behavior. Using everyday practical language, vernacular, *traditional* means *old-fashioned* or *old school*. Someone might say, for example, "Oh, she has an old-fashioned attitude!" Or maybe, "He dresses so old-fashioned!" The main strength and validity of traditional culture is that it has been passed down from generation to generation. The root may extend so many years that not even grandparents know the exact origin of the traditional culture. When children ask their parents for an explanation of a cultural practice, the response may be simply, "It's tradition!" Traditional culture promotes stability, continuity, and permanence. Traditional people generally resist change, especially rapid cultural change. What are examples of traditional Mexican culture? What is an example of a traditional Mexican resisting cultural change? What might be the reaction of "old-fashioned" traditional Mexican parents when their child decides to marry someone not Mexican? Remember that traditional culture sets parameters or boundaries that are useful guidelines. In this sense, traditional culture serves as a point of reference and point of departure.

American Popular Culture

What is meant by *American "pop" culture*? Indeed, this is very different from the traditional culture. The emphasis in pop culture is change, change, change! Culture changes constantly, and change is seen as normal. People seek out the new and the modern. What does this mean? It could be new music, new clothes/fashions, new movies, new advertisements, new furniture, new cars, new homes, new technology—the newest and latest of everything. From this perspective, the United States is a society of consumers. American capitalism is the economic system that promotes the production of products and the consumer way of life. Watching television or walking in a shopping mall, what do you see that are examples of American pop culture? In your opinion, in what ways are Mexican Americans affected and influenced by American pop culture?

American Culture

What, then, is American culture in the United States? American culture is a combination of many different historical and cultural influences. American culture includes customs, traditions, rituals, and celebrations that are unique and distinct to this country. Americans probably agree that holidays and celebrations are a major aspect of American culture. Examples include Martin Luther King Jr.'s birthday, Presidents Day, Memorial Day, Fourth of July, Labor Day, Thanksgiving, and Christmas. Does American culture also include Super Bowl Sunday, the World Series, and the Indy 500? Is it rock 'n' roll, top 40 music, McDonald's, Disneyland, Hollywood movies, and the latest television shows? After all is said and done, it appears that American culture means many things to many people. The culture of the United States is a unique blend and mixture of the history and heritage of this country.

It is intriguing to interview individuals in other countries and listen to their positive and negative perceptions of American culture including stereotypes. In your opinion, in what ways are Mexican Americans internalizing American culture and becoming Americanized? Do you feel that Mexican Americans can adhere to American culture and Mexican culture simultaneously?

Note to Students   You are invited to enroll in a wide variety of social science and humanities classes to investigate and understand American society and culture in depth.

THE STORY OF MEXICAN AMERICAN HISTORY, HERITAGE, AND CULTURE

Of the total population of the United States, there are now millions of Latinos, which translates into a significant percentage of the populace. In the Latino population, the greatest majority are people of Mexican descent. It is important to realize that Latinos are multiethnic, multicultural, and multiracial. This means that each Latin American country is an ethnic cultural group on its own. *Chilenos, Colombianos, Cubanos, Dominicanos Guatemaltecos, Mexicanos, Nicaragüenses, Puertorriqueños Salvadoreños,* and the many others are cultural groups with their own unique and distinct history, heritage, and culture. Latinos are the largest identifiable ethnic, cultural, and racial group in the United States, and they are also the fastest growing population.

Note to Students   Demography is the study of population characteristics based on data. Research the following statistical information: How many million Latinos are in the United States? What percentage of the U.S. population are Latinos? How many Latinos are in your state, and what percentage is that? How many Latinos are in your county, and what percentage is that? How many Latinos are in your city, and what percentage is that? What other demographic data are significant? See Appendix at the end of the book for U.S. census information on Latinos in the united states.

Mexican American history, heritage, and culture es una mezcla. In other words, Mexican American history and heritage is a mixture of many cultural influences going back not a few years, but thousands of years. Our story is a dynamic historical and cultural thread that follows the evolution and development of La Raza, the people. We will travel the following chronological journey: the cultural root of ancient indigenous people; the Spanish conquest of indigenous cultures; Spain's three-hundred-year colonization in New Spain; Mexican independence from Spain and the birth of a new country; the Mexican-American War; the life of Mexican Americans in Aztlán after the war; Mexican Americans in the early 1900s; the Chicano Movement; Mexican Americans in the late twentieth century; and La Raza today.

CHAPTER DISCUSSION QUESTIONS

1. What are Chicano-Latino Studies?
2. What is meant by a Chicano-Latino perspective?
3. Why is it important to know about culture?
4. Why is it important for people to understand and be knowledgeable about their cultural roots?

CHAPTER 2

ANCIENT INDIGENOUS PEOPLE:
LA GENTE INDÍGENA

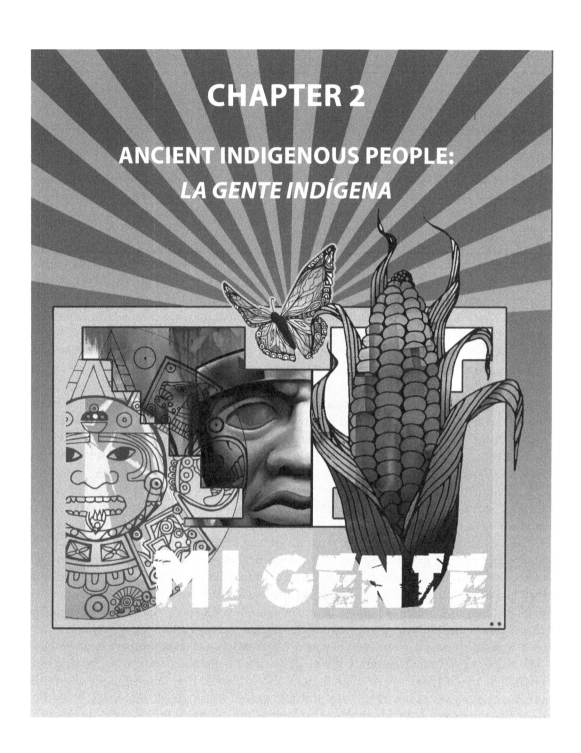

The story of *La Raza* begins with the indigenous people, *la gente indígena*. What does this mean? Why the term *indigenous*? Indigenous is not merely a term but a major concept and a perspective. Chicano-Latino Studies frequently make reference to an indigenous perspective. This perspective encompasses a cultural point of view and worldview. An indigenous perspective must be an integral part of understanding the cultural roots of *La Raza*. Any historical or contemporary analysis of Chicano-Latino culture that excludes or ignores an indigenous perspective is, by definition, incomplete.

Our narrative starts with an account of the Western Hemisphere known today as the Américas. Who were the first human beings to live here? Where did they come from? When and how did they arrive in these lands? A human epic and evolution took place over thousands of years.

This is the study of pre-Columbian América. The study examines the people who occupied the Western Hemisphere prior to the time that Columbus supposedly "discovered América." In searching for a route to the Indies, Columbus arrived in the Caribbean islands. Columbus and his men were the first Europeans on the continent, according to most popular thought. They called the inhabitants *Indians,* thinking that they had reached the Indies. The label stuck, and hundreds of years later people say in Spanish, *los indios*. From the Chicano-Latino perspective, the concept of preference is, the indigenous people, *la gente indígena*.

Indigenous refers to the first original founders and inhabitants of a land. These indigenous people were the ones who in fact "discovered América." In anthropology, the most popular explanation of the very first arrivals in the Américas is the Bering Strait theory. What is a theory? A theory is a set of ideas framed to explain the unknown. It is an educated guess and logical deduction based on the available data. Theory helps to define and clarify, and it is a point of reference and point of departure. A theory provides a set of ideas—a plausible explanation—whose strengths and weaknesses can be assessed. The Bering Strait theory holds that indigenous people migrated across a land bridge from Asia to Alaska during the Pleistocene Ice Age. Scientists argue as to whether this migration took place as early as 50,000 years ago or as late as 10,000 b.c. According to anthropologist Eric Wolf in his book *Sons of the Shaking Earth*, it probably took some 600 generations to travel the land from today's Alaska all the way down to the tip of South América.[1] This was a slow, gradual migration over thousands of years. These original discoverers of América probably did not even have a concept of what they had done. Indigenous people occupied their native land and provided names for geographical regions in their native languages. The notion of *Western Hemisphere, América,* and *New World* is the European perspective of this part of the world.

These indigenous arrivals were people of the Stone Age striving for mere survival. They were migrant people for thousands of years. They lived as nomadic wanderers, moving from place to place searching for food. As hunters and gatherers, they learned to survive under the harshest of conditions. They were probably guided by a struggle for survival based on their adaptation to a cruel physical environment. Climatic conditions beyond their control determined their fate. Food for nourishment was an overwhelming concern. What plants growing in the wild were edible? Wild berries, seeds, acorns, nopal, maguey? What animals running wild were available in the environment to hunt for food? Rabbits, deer, fish, insects, birds, mammoths? Generations of experience based on trial and error taught them to use and appreciate the flora and fauna, plants and animals. Survival itself was a major accomplishment. And notwithstanding the human concern, they learned to beware of the predators! The ways and means they used to adapt to their harsh environment are called *ecological adaptation*. It is unimaginable what men and women had to overcome during this time period.

Note to Students   For an excellent visual presentation that depicts the life of indigenous people during this epoch, Google: history channel: journey to 10,000 B.C. A description of the program states:

> *Viewers will go back in time to when early humans are just starting to inhabit North America and huge climate fluctuations cause a mini-Ice Age. The saber tooth cat, the giant ground sloth and the woolly mammoth are suddenly becoming extinct. How does man survive? Travel to early archaeological sites in North America and watch as scientists uncover fossilized bones, ancient homes and weapons of stone.*

Also included in the program are new theoretical ideas that present a different perspective on the Bering Strait theory.

MESOAMÉRICA

The cultures and civilizations of this chapter focus on Mesoamérica. The geographical location generally covers central México and Central América. Within this region, indigenous people attained an incredible level of civilization. The ancient world of Mesoamérica is a source of wonder to this day.

As previously stated, indigenous people had a nomadic lifestyle for thousands of years. How did people graduate from nomadic wanderers, hunters, and gatherers to a higher, more sophisticated mode of existence and lifestyle? Gradually, a revolutionary change occurred in their way of living that affected their life forever. This became known as the *Agricultural Revolution.*

How did the Agricultural Revolution change their lives? With farming and irrigation, people were able to grow their own crops. It revolved around the domestication of plants, and it occurred slowly over the millennia. This required the intelligence to identify desirable plants and seeds. Learning to cultivate was an art and science. This was no little accomplishment, but instead a huge step forward for humankind. The domestication of plants provided for a stable food supply. As in previous generations, they no longer had to wander and migrate from place to place in search of food. Agriculture provided the people an opportunity to develop a settled way of life or sedentism. With the cultivation of crops developed a sedentary lifestyle and permanent settlements springing up in the best agricultural areas. The power of plants, fruits, and vegetables—what an awesome power to control for the first time in human history! Villages and towns became commonplace. A stable food supply also meant a revolution in the concept of time in daily life. Some people were now free to think and wonder. The Agricultural Revolution made it possible for men and women to expand and refine their culture.

The key to understanding the development of agriculture and irrigation in Mesoamérica is the domestication of corn. Corn was unknown in the rest of the world until it was cultivated by the indigenous people. Years ago, scientists asked the research question, What is the specific location where corn was first domesticated? They circled and circled the Américas and identified several locations. Scientists finally came upon a little valley in central México known as the Tehuacán Valley, *Valle de Tehuacán,* located in the state of Puebla. After several seasons of excavation, it was finally determined to be the place where corn agriculture began, about 5000 to 7000 B.C. Farming and irrigation after about 2000 B.C. was commonplace in fertile areas.

From the Chicano-Latino perspective, the importance of corn cultivation and agriculture cannot be emphasized enough. This was a revolutionary discovery. Just as microchips and computers have revolutionized the world today, agriculture revolutionized indigenous culture. Thousands of years later, we see the many uses of corn and corn products now in our daily life. Not only was it corn but many other agricultural crops. This included varieties of beans, *chiles,* potatoes, tomatoes, squash, pumpkins, yams, peanuts, cashew nuts, sunflowers, avocados, strawberries, pineapples, and many more. The Inca in Perú are especially known for their ingenuity in domesticating a large variety of potatoes. The indigenous people developed the process for making maple syrup, vanilla, and chocolate. It is intriguing to discover how the Maya came up with the process for chocolate. It goes without saying that today, all these food products feed the world and are a huge part of the global economy.

Note to Students To learn more about the discovery of chocolate, go to http://www. nationalgeographic.com and see the story "Ancient Chocolate Found in Maya 'Teapot.'"

The indigenous people contributed these crops to the world. When the Spanish arrived in the New World, they were amazed and intrigued by the great assortments of foods, fruits, and vegetables in the diet of the indigenous people. These fruits and vegetables were then exported by the Spanish to Spain and from Spain to the rest of Europe and the world. From the indigenous perspective, these ancient people deserve the credit, acknowledgment, and recognition for their major contribution. It is unfortunate that people still harbor prejudice and negative stereotypes, such as, "Indians were a bunch of wild savages running around naked, shooting with bow and arrows." Quite the contrary; they had the intelligence to create civilizations that amaze the world to this day. The indigenous people unleashed their creativity and imagination in the creation of culture and civilization.

We should also appreciate the many beautiful flowers that were domesticated in the Américas by the indigenous people. A perfect example is illustrated by José Antonio Burciaga in his book *Drink Cultura, Chicanismo*. The poinsettia Christmas flower is very popular in the United States. In truth, the plant is a Mexican flower called *cuetlaxochitl* by the Aztecs. Burciaga states:

> *The cuetlaxochitl was cultivated as an exotic gift from nature and admired but never touched. Its bright red color had been given by some god as a reminder of the periodic sacrificial offerings in accordance with the creation of the Fifth Sun. . . . Five hundred years after the encounter between Europe and this continent, we should attempt to recapture the history and contributions of the indigenous peoples. It would be a noble act to give the flower its original name, cuetlaxochitl—"flower that withers, flower that perishes like all that is pure"—as a reminder of wounded Mother Earth.[2]*

The indigenous perspective relates a philosophy of respect and appreciation for the natural order. Philosophically, it is a profound awareness of the dynamic equilibrium among humankind, nature, and the universe.

During the pre-Columbian era, there were hundreds of indigenous cultures. In fact, their descendants still live today throughout the Américas. The following sections provide a brief description and introduction to a small sample of these people. We can see these groups as a reflection of the many accomplishments and achievements of the indigenous people as a whole.

Olmeca

Of the many civilizations of Mesoamérica, chronologically the first one of major impact and influence is the Olmec, *Olmeca*. As the parent of future generations of cultures, the Olmec are called the Mother Culture, *la cultura madre*. The center of the Olmec civilization was the region of today's Veracruz, México. Their power and influence spread for many hundreds of miles in all directions. Actually, Ignacio Bernal, in his book *The Olmec World*, states, "The Olmec zone covered a total of about 7,000 square miles."[3] This means the cultural influence of these people was indeed extensive. At their height, Olmec civilization existed from about the 1200s B.C. to around the 100s B.C.

A series of scientific expeditions in the early 1900s to Veracruz could not have been more amazing. Gigantic stone heads averaging 18 tons were discovered. The source of the stone used could only be from miles away. Over a dozen of these colossal stone heads have been found. The face of a person is carved on each of these huge boulders. The name *Olmec* was given to the newly discovered people. Other findings at Olmec archaeological sites include pottery, figurines, and *stelae*, inscribed stone slabs.

Clearly, the Olmec were intellectuals. They are credited with the concept of zero in the New World. Zero, as a place holder, is the key to a mathematical system. Unlike our base-10 or decimal system, they used a vigesimal system, base-20. With their counting system, the Olmec could calculate everything from simple arithmetic to advanced math. Apparently, future cultures and civilizations used Olmec mathematical concepts to do science, architecture, engineering, and building construction.

The Olmec contemplated the concept of time. Similar to the concept of zero and a mathematical system, understanding the concept of time is characteristic of advanced cognitive thinking and the power of conceptualization. They invented a system for measuring time. Chronology is the science of developing a system to accurately measure time intervals. This means keeping the time of day. It also involves inventing an accurate calendar to record days, weeks, months, years, centuries, and millennia. It is as though the Olmec were obsessed with the concept of time, or at least, it was a major preoccupation.

To study these ancient indigenous people is to have more questions than answers, the mystery of the Olmec. What happened to the Olmec civilization? Why were their ceremonial sites abandoned? Educated guesses abound, but no one knows for sure. New discoveries await as research continues.

An example of a new discovery was reported in 2006 by *New York Times* writer John Noble Wilford. The headline reads: "Stone discovered with 3,000-year-old unknown script." He reports: "A stone slab bearing 3,000-year-old writing previously unknown to scholars has been found in the Mexican state of Veracruz, and archaeologists say it is an example of the oldest script ever discovered in the Western Hemisphere." The discovery was by archaeologists Carmen Rodriguez Martinez of the National Institute of Anthropology and History of México and Ponciano Ortiz Ceballos of Vera Cruz University.[4] This demonstrates that there are many treasures in the Américas waiting to be found.

Note to Students   Do research and learn the progress of deciphering this unknown newly discovered Olmec writing.

Today, we look back and marvel at the ingenuity, creativity, and imagination of the Olmec, *los Olmeca, la cultura madre.* Their cultural influence continued for centuries. As Ignacio

© Jo Ann Snover, 2013. Used under license from Shutterstock, Inc. Mayan observatory

Bernal states, "The end of the Olmec world is not an end but a beginning. It leads directly into the Classic world of Teotihuacán, Monte Alban, Tajín, and the Maya. These people were to absorb the Olmec inheritance and push civilization to far higher levels. They would reach a new ledge on the rocky ascent to civilization."[5]

Maya

The Maya civilization spanned a period of over a thousand years and covered a huge geographical region. The ancient Maya lived in today's southern México, the Yucatán Peninsula, and Central América. The time period of the Maya went from the early classic, late classic, to the post classic, which is approximately from the 200s to 1200s A.D.

Who were the Maya? What inspired their soaring culture? The Maya reached a high level of civilization and culture rarely attained by humankind. What were the accomplishments and achievements of the Maya? These are intriguing characteristics of their life, culture, and society over a lengthy time span of many generations:

Agriculture

Astronomy

Architecture

Art and science of health and medicine

This includes what today are called folk healers, *curanderos* and *curanderas*.

Art, music, dance, literature, poetry

Building construction

This included all sorts of design and construction—buildings, bridges, pathways, streets, waterways, and waterworks.

Cities of many thousands of residents

Of course some people lived in small towns, villages, and in the countryside.

City planning

Urban and rural planning was necessary in order to lay out cities in an organized and effective configuration. This included city districts and zones, such as residential areas; business, trade, and commerce districts; the farmers' market, *mercado*; and agricultural zones.

Engineering in many fields of specialty

Today we may call these specialties—for example, architectural, civil, environmental, mining, surveying, and water engineering.

Irrigation

Mathematics

Philosophy

Pyramids

Religion

Sculpture

Writing, books, and libraries

The Maya were intellectual giants. Maya religion, art, philosophy, science, and learning were closely intertwined. They were master builders and artists. Their pyramids were magnificent in scope and design. Maya astronomy was surprisingly accurate. Only centuries of patient recordkeeping could account for their knowledge of the moon, sun, and stars. They developed an accurate solar calendar. Who could question the Maya leader who could predict when a shadow would appear before the moon or the sun would disappear? At the time when Europe fell into the Dark Ages, Maya intellect soared.

The mystery of the Maya revolves around questions regarding the rise and fall of this great civilization. War, revolution, internal upheaval, one or all may have been the cause of their downfall. All we know is that at a certain time, their beautiful cities and sacred sites were abandoned. The jungle reclaimed its buildings, monuments, and pyramids with the wild vegetation of the mighty rainforest. With the study of this magnificent civilization we are learning how men and women rose to a lofty pinnacle seldom seen by humankind. The beauty of the situation is that the ancient Maya will never be forgotten and their direct descendants live in Mesoamérica today.

Note to Students   Students are encouraged to go online to see the many glorious and magnificent pyramids and archaeological sites of the Maya. A few examples include Bonampak, Chichén-Itza (including the astronomical observatory), Copán, Palenque, Tajín, Tikal, Tulum, and Uxmal.

Teotihuacanos

Another great ancient indigenous civilization is Teotihuacán and the people called Teotihuacanos. This archaeological site is located some thirty miles northeast of México City. This sacred site is referred to as the *City of the Gods*. It is the location of the Pyramid of the Sun, a massive pyramid, and the largest in central México. Adjacent is the Street of the Dead, leading to the Pyramid of the Moon. The third major pyramid is the Feathered Serpent. It is estimated that the height of the civilization was approximately from the late 100s to about 600s or 700s A.D. Perhaps some 100,000 to maybe 200,000 people lived in this area during its zenith. The downfall of Teotihuacán is the subject of much debate and controversy. Was it war, invasion, revolution, internal upheaval, political unrest, drought, one or all? There are many theories, and the research continues.

Teotihuacán

Pictured in the forefront is Professor Matt Espinoza Watson

The purpose of this chapter is merely to provide a brief introduction to the spectacular history, heritage, and culture of the Olmeca, Maya, and Teotihuacanos. There were countless cultures too numerous to include in this brief overview—such as the Tolteca, Mixteca, and Zapoteca. For the serious student, there are many books and media available for study. Thousands of tourists visit awesome archaeological locations and sacred sites throughout Mesoamérica. When visiting a site, you may notice scientists from all over the world continuing to do excavations. Many questions remain to be answered concerning these amazing and enigmatic civilizations.

THE STORY OF THE AZTECA, MEXICA

The Azteca were the last of the great Mesoamerican empires. The story of the Azteca begins with their legendary homeland. These indigenous people lived in the faraway place of Aztlán (Azatatlán). From the Chicano-Latino perspective and the Chicano Movement of the 1960s, the Southwest of the United States was proclaimed Aztlán. Supposedly, due to earthquakes, drought, and famine, they decided to leave their homeland and journey south. The departure from Aztlán was probably about the early 1100s a.d. They traveled a long way, searching for a place to settle.

The Azteca arrived in the Valley of México, *Valle de Anáhuac.* This may have been about the mid-1200s. It turned out to be a series of islands in the middle of a series of lakes. They were in search of a sign—an eagle, perched on a cactus with a serpent in its beak—that would indicate they were in the right place. Finally, the omen and the prophecy came to pass. (This is the symbol seen in the middle of the Mexican flag.) After much strife, conflict, trials and tribulations, and even bloodshed, they settled on a swampy island. On Lake Texcoco they established Tenochtitlán, the Azteca capitol.

The Azteca built a massive empire and confederation overseeing millions of people. The Azteca were also known as the Mexica (pronounced "Mesheeka"). Their language was Náhuatl. Slowly but surely, they developed their unique culture, society, and civilization.

The Azteca were master engineers and architects; thus, they built causeways or bridges from the mainland to Tenochtitlán. They also built magnificent aqueducts to provide fresh water for the large populace. Dams and dikes were built to preserve the city. Relay runners delivered mail throughout. This could only be described as a robust metropolitan city.

Agriculture to feed a large population was a major endeavor. As the populace increased and land became limited, the people of Tenochtitlán developed an ingenious method of growing crops. These were *chinampas*, floating gardens. People constructed rafts made from wooden branches. They piled them with dirt and mud. On this raft they planted and grew their fruits and vegetables. Today, visitors can visit vestiges of the floating gardens, *los jardines flotantes,* in Xochimilco, Distrito Federal, México.

Azteca society and culture were stratified into different aspects of daily life. People involved themselves in various groups and communities. Social stratification meant that within society, people were in social classes based on jobs, professions, status, and prestige. Based on this, people went to different schools and colleges.

This is a brief example of the stratification in the daily life of the Azteca:

Calmecac	College and monastery school for priests and leaders
Calpulli	Self-sustaining units of land owned by a family group with set boundaries, granting full rights for growing, hunting, fishing, and livelihood
Cuicacalli	School for women, especially giving the noblewoman an opportunity to become a priestess (house of songs)
Macequales	Members of calpullis
Mayeques	Group of natives, similar to serfs, with few if any rights
Pipiltin	Members of certain calpulli, who became the ruling class
Pochteca	Buyers, traders, merchants (not agrarian farmers)
Tectecuhtin	Persons who served their society as warriors
Telpochcalli	Training center for the warriors
Tlatoques	Persons elected to serve as orators for each calpulli
Tlacotin	Persons who indentured themselves to rulers as laborers

In a highly advanced civilization, people were required to perform a large variety of functions that were necessary for an organized society. These ranged from homemakers to leaders, priests, warriors, scientists, farmers, artists, philosophers, and anyone else needed. This is called the *social organization* of society and culture.

During pre-Columbian times, indigenous México had a population of major proportions. According to *The Course of Mexican History* by Meyer, Sherman, and Deeds, "If, as some authorities believe, all of Mexico had a population approaching 30 million, it was more populous than any country in Europe. France, the largest, had about 20 million, and Spain, 10 at most." And in regard to Tenochtitlán, "Even with the more conservative estimate of 150,000 to 200,000 residents accepted by most scholars, the Aztec capital was one of the largest cities in the world."[6] The arts and humanities were most important in the daily lives of the Azteca. Art, music, dance, literature, and philosophy were human endeavors that embellished the quality of life. The philosophical ideas and perspectives they developed are especially fascinating and intriguing. In *Aztec Thought and Culture*, Miguel León-Portilla quotes the philosopher and poet Nezahualcóyotl:

A poem attributed to the famous Nezahualcóyotl questions the possibility of finding satisfaction in earthly things:

What does your mind seek?
Where is your heart?
If you give your heart to each and every thing,
you lead it nowhere: you destroy your heart.
Can anything be found on earth?

. . .

Truly do we live on earth?
Not forever on earth; only a little while here.
Although it be jade, it will be broken,
Although it be gold, it is crushed,
Although it be quetzal feather, it is torn asunder.
Not forever on earth; only a little while here.[7]

Indigenous philosophical schools of thought dealt with the full range of human concerns and the human condition. This included birth, life, death, mortality, spiritualism, destiny, meaning, wisdom, reality, existence, creation, the Creator, the heavens, earth, and the universe.

Note to Students For an intriguing visual graphic of Tenochtitlán, go to the History Channel and the program titled "Engineering an Empire: The Aztecs." According to this program, the Aztec empire covered an area of tens of thousands of square miles and included many millions of subjects.

A CHICANO-LATINO PERSPECTIVE ON THE STUDY OF INDIGENOUS HISTORY, HERITAGE, AND CULTURE

Why study the indigenous cultural roots? This may be a perplexing and bewildering question. Chicano-Latino Studies Professor Matt Espinoza Watson, JD, provides this insight and reflection:

The Importance of Indigenous Thought & Culture to 21st century Chican@s

Learning about the civilizations of ancient Mexico can change you. That's a warning and a challenge: On one hand, it is like looking into the mirror, and seeing an ancient reflection of yourself through your ancestors. It's learning that our history is not just crossing borders; it goes far deeper than just the history of Mexicanos in the U.S. But it also gives us the idea that migrations have been a part of our history for thousands of years. It gives us a different way of looking at ourselves, our culture, and the world around us.

It's learning that the treasures of ancient Mexico were not carried off by Cortes and the Conquistadores, but are still here with us in the teachings, myths, poetry, art and legends of the Mexica, Maya, Olmecatl, and Toltecatl. It's also understanding that these treasures are universal, and have something for everyone, regardless of where your own ancestors are from.

Learning about America before the arrival of Europeans can open many doors. For most of us, our education simply left out anything about the achievements of these remarkable civilizations. If we've heard anything, it's that they were bloodthirsty savages (a view reinforced recently through Mel Gibson's Apocalypto). We don't hear that our ancestors were living in cities of 200,000 while Europe was in the dark ages (the first cities on the American continent); that the calendars developed in ancient Mexico more than 2000 years ago are more accurate than any other calendar developed by any *people at* any *point in recorded history (including the Gregorian calendar, which we use today). We don't hear about the highly advanced architects, astronomers, mathematicians, botanists, farmers, sculptors, warriors and poets that flourished in ancient Mexico. And because we don't hear this, we don't know a part of ourselves, and we underestimate our own potential.*

We lack roots in many ways. As we are more 'connected' to each other through technology, we are less connected with ourselves and our past. Our experiences of nature are few & far between. We can begin to reconnect though. There is knowledge here that helps us understand the world around us, from the stars and solar system, to the very principles of life itself and the mysteries of the beyond. Some of us speak Spanish, some are still immersed in Mexican culture within the U.S., while others of us are generations removed from Mexico and any type of ancestral knowledge of our past. Most of us have lost the connection to these civilizations, and with it, lost a part of ourselves. The part of ourselves that is the knowledge of our great great grandparents and ancestors, that helps us see ourselves properly & know who we are. As one former student put it, "we're still trying to rub the brown off of our skin in many ways because we're not hearing the voices of our past; communication of that sort is a medicine and we have to take it and learn from it in order to start decolonizing ourselves."

At the same time, even the most far removed of us still have ties to these ancient civilizations: Every time you mention "chocolate," "tomato," or an "avocado," you are using the language of the Aztecs. Every time you eat a taco or a tortilla chip or popcorn, you are connecting to one of the remarkable achievements of your ancestors: inventing corn. Long before Genetically Engineered organisms, ancient Mexican plant scientists cross-bred a grass that was of no use to humans into a highly nutritious & adaptable food that would be the basis of civilizations all over the continent, and later, the world.

In a time of rapid changes in the world around us, the calendars of Ancient Mexico seem to forecast even greater changes in the years to come. Are they simply relics of the past, or do they point to the massive changes that need to be made to survive as humans on planet Earth? Knowledge that at first seems very far removed from our current life circumstances can begin to seem surprisingly relevant & useful for us, in this generation, with just a bit of reflection. What did they know that we don't? The answer is, a whole lot. . . .

In this country we're taught Mexicans are foreigners who don't belong here, that Mexicans aren't intelligent, and many of us come to believe it, because we haven't heard any different. But armed with the power of the knowledge of our ancestors, we can reclaim our future and take our rightful place as leaders within this society. As a mural in the Zapatista community of La Realidad says, "En el presente se estudia el pasado para ver hacia el futuro." (In the present we study the past to look toward the future.) As we look to the past, we can hear the words of the last tlatoani, or leader of the Mexica (Aztecs), named Cuauhtemoc,

Timeline—Pre-Columbian América

Ice Age	5000–7000 Tehuacán Valley Corn domestication Domestication of plants, fruits and vegetables	Olmeca 1200's–100's
		0

B.C. A.D.

Maya 200's–900's	Azteca–Mexica 1200's–1519

200's–800's Teotihuacán	1519–21 Spanish Conquest

900's–1200's
Tolteca
@ city of Tula

Quetzalcóatl

who left a message for us as the great city of Tenochtitlán lay in ruins: "Our beloved sun has disappeared and has left us in total darkness. But we know that it will again return, will again come out and will come anew to shine upon us . . . Now we deliver the task to our children that they guard our writings and our knowledge. . . . And do not forget to inform our children intensely how it will be. How we will rise! How the destiny of our beloved motherland Anahuak will be realized and how we will help it fulfill its grand destiny." There are many that think that the dawning of the sixth sun, that Cuauhtemoc spoke of, is upon us. Will we rise to the occasion? Let us begin looking toward the future now, by learning about our past. . . .

CHAPTER DISCUSSION QUESTIONS

1. Discuss the history, heritage, and culture of *la gente indígena*.
2. What were the major achievements and accomplishments of the ancient indigenous civilizations?
3. What was happening in Europe during the time of the Olmeca to the Azteca?
4. What is the cultural influence of *la gente indígena* for Mexican Americans and Latinos today?

5. Research the following. The date December 21, 2012, is a crucial and intriguing event in the Maya calendar. Why was the concept of time important to the Maya?

© Betacam-SP/Shutterstock.com

CHAPTER 3

THE SPANISH CONQUEST, 1519 TO 1521, AND SPANISH COLONIZATION, 1521 TO 1821

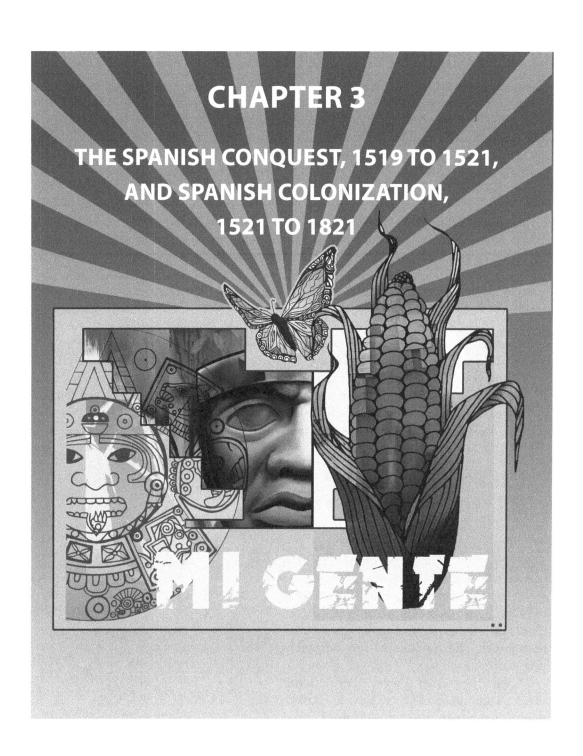

IN 1492, COLUMBUS SAILED THE OCEAN BLUE

Christopher Columbus, otherwise known as *Cristóbal Colón*, is a very interesting historical character and protagonist. The topic of Columbus is a very serious issue in Chicano-Latino history and heritage. However, an anonymous writer presents a satire of the situation with the following account. Imagine watching this on your television nightly news:

BREAKING NEWS! REPORT, OCTOBER 12, 1492. News Flash:

The news was received and confirmed by satellite image that, during his star trek, Columbus Discovered América! He and his men encountered strange animal-like creatures resembling human beings . . . Indians . . . living naked on exotic beaches and jungles . . . gibbering weird sounds . . . eating weird food . . . worshiping weird pagan gods. Chris will round up and chain a few of these savage creatures . . . along with their gold and silver trinkets and be back in the City late next month. The Mayor's office is sparing no expense planning the first ever "Columbus Day Parade." Several Hollywood stars have confirmed attendance at the reception gala event, which will be a glamorous pic opportunity for the paparazzi. The Hispanic Chamber of Commerce declared that Columbus Day will be a huge boom for business. The Chamber will offer a variety of business workshops that will assist entrepreneurs in making a killing from the discovery of América. According to our country's president, this promises to be a very profitable holiday for generations to come. Christopher's new book, Discover América for Dummies, *will be in bookstores this spring and is predicted to be an instant bestseller.*

This is Jonathane Goodman with your NNBC nightly news.

Please stay tuned for the Night Show with Jay Leno.

Of course this *BREAKING NEWS* report is a lark! From the European perspective, Columbus was a brave and courageous explorer who went where no man had gone before. As it turns out, Columbus was the precursor to the Spanish Conquest. This means that he set the stage for the invasion and conquest of the indigenous people of the Américas.

Columbus created a legacy that has survived for hundreds of years. How is Christopher Columbus seen today in Spain, Europe, the United States, and Latin América? Who celebrates Columbus Day? In Chicano-Latino Studies, it is crucial to present the indigenous perspective. Do the indigenous people celebrate Columbus Day? Could it be that indigenous people celebrating Columbus Day would be like the Jewish celebrating the birthday of Adolf Hitler? These are questions to ponder in the long, involved process of examining hundreds of years of Chicano-Latino history, heritage, and culture.

From the Chicano-Latino perspective, Columbus is a controversial historical figure, to say the least. An interesting example of this controversy is presented by *Culture Clash*. They are a Chicano comedy group that sprang from the Chicano Movement, and they are masters at what is called Chicano *teatro*, theater. The performances of *Culture Clash* are a satirical masterpiece. In their video titled *A Bowl of Beings*, they present an intriguing satire on Christopher Columbus. In this spoof, Columbus is a great explorer but accused of murdering *América*. Like the caper news report, this satire challenges the audience to ponder the far-reaching implications of the Spanish invasion and the war of the worlds.

<u>Note to Students</u>   Student interested in learning more about this professional theatrical group should visit http://www.cultureclash.com.

SPANISH CONQUEST, *LA CONQUISTA*, 1519 TO 1521: SPANISH GENOCIDE OF THE INDIGENOUS AZTECA, MEXICA

In 1519, Moctezuma II, the Azteca emperor, felt a sense of impending doom. A mysterious comet was looming in the sky. There were reported sightings from the Gulf of México of *mountains that move* in the ocean spewing thunder and lightning. Coming from the *mountains that move* were seen strange four-legged creatures with the body of a man. Unbeknown to Moctezuma, Hernán Cortés was on his way that very moment to conquer the Azteca. A potent prophecy persisted that the Tolteca god Quetzalcóatl, Feathered Serpent, would return from the direction of the rising sun. Many years prior, perhaps about 947 A.D., Quetzalcóatl was born by the name of Ce Acatl Topiltzin, meaning "One Reed" and "Our Prince." He became king and established his reign in the city of Tula (some fifty miles northwest of today's México City). Due to a misdeed, he exiled himself. Later, he was deified and became a god, promising to return in all his glory and reclaim his throne. Apparently, Moctezuma believed in the prophecy that Quetzalcóatl would return in 1519—*Ce Acatl*, which is "One Reed," according to the Aztec year. The unscrupulous Hernán Cortés would take ruthless advantage of this prophecy and conquer the Azteca in less than two years.

Hernán Cortés and his soldiers made their grand entrance into the metropolitan city of Tenochtitlán. They were in awe of the marvelous, beautiful, splendid city before them. The people welcomed them as the arrival of gods and showered them with gifts of all sorts. Ignacio Bernal, in *Mexico Before Cortez: Art, History, Legend*, describes the first meeting between Cortés and Moctezuma:

And when Cortez saw and understood and when they told him that the great Moctezuma was coming, he got down from his horse, and as soon as he was near Moctezuma they simultaneously paid great reverence to each other. Moctezuma welcomed him and our Cortez replied through doña Marina wishing him very good health. And it seems to me that Cortez, through the tongue of doña Marina who was by his side, offered his right hand and Moctezuma did not wish to take it, but he did give his hand to Cortez. And then Cortez brought out a necklace which he had ready at hand, made of glass stones that I have already said are called margaritas, which contained intricate patterns and many colors, and the stones were strung [on] gold cords and with musk so that the necklace should have a sweet scent, and strung it around the neck of the great Moctezuma, and when he had placed it there he was about to embrace him, and those great lords who accompanied Moctezuma held back the arm of Cortez so that he should not embrace him, for they considered it an indignity.1

Moctezuma was painfully unaware that his fate and that of his civilization had been sealed. How could Moctezuma know that a strange set of circumstances brought this stranger from across the ocean to the door of the Azteca empire?

Cortés was greatly aided by the Indian woman Doña Marina, his translator, mistress, and confidante. She kept him informed of crucial information, making it possible for him to succeed with his mission. She bore Cortés a son, Don Martín. Doña Marina was also known as La Malinche. Today, there is much controversy and debate regarding her role in the conquest. Should Doña Marina be considered a great woman and heroine? Should she be portrayed as a back-stabbing traitor for allying herself with Hernán Cortés, the invader and conqueror? She is a very enigmatic character in contemporary Chicana-Latina literature.

As it turns out, the Spanish conquerors, *conquistadores*, came into the Azteca civilization with a Christian cross in one hand and a metal sword in the other. Most would agree that the Spanish were militarily superior. They possessed metal weapons, guns, and cannons. The Spanish were merciless in battle and were famous for their vicious fighting dogs. Cortés quickly became an expert at divide and conquer as he rallied indigenous people to fight against the Azteca.

There is a famous episode known as the Sad Night, *la noche triste*. While Cortés was away at the coast at Veracruz, Captain Pedro de Alvarado attacked and killed Azteca leaders who were taking part in a religious ceremony. Cortés returned to Tenochtitlán and a battle ensued. Seeing their tenuous situation, Cortés and his men fled in the shadow of darkness but were discovered and attacked. After many casualties, Cortés and some of his men barely escaped the city with their lives. It is said that Cortés sat under a tree and cried for the loss of his men on that day of July 1, 1520.

By no means were the Spanish done, however. They reorganized and planned the siege of the city with the help of their Indian, *indio*, allies. The Spanish successfully surrounded the island city of Tenochtitlán. They blocked the causeways, cutting off the food supply. They destroyed the aqueducts that delivered fresh water to the island. Effectively strangling the city, they moved methodically, slaughtering the population. Led by the unscrupulous Cortés, they destroyed and burned Tenochtitlán. The conquest of the Azteca was a bloodbath and a holocaust. Besides the military assault, the majority of Aztecas died from the diseases that came with the Spanish. Even though Aztecas had an art and science of medicine, it was not strong enough to guard against the European plagues such as smallpox.

Interest still persists as to the death of Moctezuma. When the Spanish declared their hostile intentions, Moctezuma was captured and held prisoner in his own palace by Cortés. Moctezuma appeared indecisive as a leader. One version of his death is that Moctezuma was stoned and killed by his own people as he tried to address them from his palace. This may have been intentional or unintentional, as stones started flying in the confusion. It may be that Aztecas were bewildered by his inability to protect them against the alien invaders. Another story says that Cortés had him killed. Yet another version is a story of the oral cultural tradition. This recounts that Moctezuma died of a broken heart! This is probably meant symbolically. This version of the story may be someone's cultural fabrication! Regardless of the exact cause of death, did he hold himself ultimately responsible for the destruction of his people? Moctezuma, the emperor who engineered a great civilization, was dead.

Cuauhtémoc, at the age of 18, was the last and final emperor of the Azteca. He fomented a resistance, but resistance was futile. Cuauhtémoc was finally tortured and hung. He was killed and the Azteca Empire destroyed. This had been one of the greatest civilizations in the world. From the indigenous perspective, Cuauhtémoc was and is viewed as a cultural hero.

This is the birth of Mexican cultural roots. Over Tenochtitlán, Cortés and the Spanish placed today's modern México City, *la ciudad de México*. Despite the conquest, indigenous culture is alive and well. A unique perspective is stated in *Drink Cultura, Chicanismo*, by José Antonio Burciaga: "I refer to a mural in Mérida, Yucatán. It depicts a battle scene between Mayan Indians and Spanish soldiers. Underneath is a plaque with the words '. . . they conquered us, but our culture conquered them.'"[2] Yes, the indigenous people were invaded and conquered. However, when all came to pass, the rich indigenous cultural roots conquered all. The indigenous culture is an integral dimension of the lives of Mexicans and Latinos today.

Note to Students   Research. As mentioned, the conquest was a holocaust and bloodbath. Google: no quiero ir al ciela, augusto g. menocal. The late Menocal is a Cuban artist. The title of one of his works is *No Quiero Ir Al Cielo*. In the painting, the artist portrays a proud

Nueva España

1521 ●●●●●●●●●●●●●●●●●●●●●●●●●●●●●●●●● 1810

1519–21	1500's	1600's	1700's	1800's	1810–21 *México*
Spanish Conquest					1810–21 Period of Mexican Independence

indio about to be burned alive by the *conquistadores*. It appears the Christian priests are ministering to him and contemplating his death. It is a very powerful scene that evokes a strong emotional reaction. This painting represents the story of *La Conquista* from the indigenous perspective. You can see this painting at the *Museo Nacional de Bellas Artes* in Havana, Cuba.

SPANISH COLONIZATION OF NEW SPAIN, *NUEVA ESPAÑA*, 1521–1810

Welcome! *¡Bienvenidos!* The Spanish welcomed themselves to the Western Hemisphere! They initially came into the Caribbean islands and spread into the Yucatán Península. A pivotal point was their move into central México with the conquest of the Azteca. Subsequently, Spaniards explored further up in North America, and others journeyed downward into Central and South América. This was the period of "Spanish exploration." From the perspective of Spain, these lands were Spanish colonies. The sprawling territories of *Nueva España* were huge. The Spanish explored the lands that today extend from Florida, to the Midwest of the United States, to California and all the way down to the tip of South América (with the exception of Brazil, colonized by Portugal). As they traversed this vast area, the Spaniards ignored or deleted the indigenous names for the geographical locations and named the areas in Spanish. Some names of locations survived in an indigenous language.

Note to Students   Examine a map of México and Latin América to identify names in the indigenous languages.

Nueva España and the period of Spanish colonization lasted three hundred years. This is called the colonial period of Latin América. In reference to México, this is called the period of colonial México. The Spanish were the victors and the indigenous people the vanquished. The invaders were the colonizers and the others were the colonized and oppressed. The Spanish raped the indigenous culture and committed cultural genocide. Spain took control of the land and the indigenous people were relegated to second-class people and strangers in their own land. From the indigenous perspective, the arrival of the Spanish in the Américas was an invasion of aliens from another world.

This was a period of Spanish exploitation of the indigenous people. *La gente indígena* were forced into slave labor for all these years. The indigenous people became the peons, *peones*, doing all the necessary labor in this society of New Spain. This work included all types of jobs from the kitchen to construction to arts and crafts. Indigenous peons labored in agriculture, farming, and ranching.

A major enterprise for the Spanish involved their insatiable hunger for silver and gold. The indigenous people were enslaved and forced to mine silver, gold, and other metal with picks and shovels and bare hands. Ships, or Spanish galleons, departed from the New World loaded down with gold and silver, headed for Spain. An example of one of these sunken

Spanish ships was found in 1985 with $450 million in treasure! Another sunken ship was found afterward with even more riches. Treasure hunters continue to seek out ships at the bottom of the Caribbean. The ghosts of history surely reside in these old sunken Spanish galleons.

**Note to Students** If interested in learning of the discovery of treasure ships, go online to the Mel Fisher Maritime Heritage Society and Historical Museum in Key West, Florida.

Cultural Clash and the Birth of Racism

The Spanish established a new social and cultural organization in _Nueva España_. This was the territory that later became México and Latin América. The king and queen of Spain with their monarchy and royal families oversaw the colonies in América. In Europe, this was the time of the feudal land system. This meant that landlords owned and managed the land. The peasantry were the peons destined to do the slave labor. Landlords controlled the labor, and that created their wealth. The European feudal land system was transplanted and established in the New World. As in many societies, the government and social structure were controlled by those with land, wealth, status, and prestige. A system of social power and influence was developed with a hierarchy. The following is the general framework of this hierarchical order:

Españoles. Spanish born in Spain. These Spanish born in the mother country were on the top of the social and cultural power structure. They were called _Peninsulares_, meaning Spanish arrivals from Spain and the Spanish peninsula. The _peninsulares_ saw themselves as purebloods directly from the motherland. _Peninsulares_ were Eurocentric because from their worldview, Europe was the center of the universe. They were also very ethnocentric, meaning that they considered themselves socially and culturally superior. Spanish ethnocentrism became an integral part of the society and culture. The Spanish from Spain were also called _Gachupines. Gachupín_ was used as a somewhat derogatory label by some people in the colonies.

Criollos. These were the Spaniards born in the New World. The _criollos_ were not born in the motherland and therefore were below the status and prestige of the _peninsulares_.

Mestizos. These were the people of mixed Spanish and Indian blood. _Mestizos_ were destined to be the majority group in _Latino América_ years later.

Los Indios. The people of pure Indian blood, _la gente indígena,_ became the peasantry or peons of the society. The indigenous people were on the bottom of the social structure and social order.

In most cases, the European feudal land system involved Europeans oppressing Europeans. The landlords were Europeans and the peons were also Europeans. Europeans oppressed their own people due to their feudal land system. However, in New Spain, there was a marked racial difference between the landlords and the peons clearly based on racial discrimination and inequality. In this society, the landlords, *hacendados*, were Spanish Europeans or *criollos*. The peons were *indios* and *mestizos* living and laboring on the land of the landlord. The *hacendados* owned large estates called *haciendas,* and this was the *hacienda* system. Of course the Spanish confiscated the best of the lands for themselves and ignored undesirable territory. Spaniards established a social and cultural system where Spanish ethnocentrism was the norm and the dominant ideology. Dominant ideology meant that the social and cultural norms and ruling ideas were established by the dominant group—in this case, the Spanish. This racial divide between *españoles, mestizos,* and *indios* had dire consequences for years to come.

Birth and Cultural Roots of *La Raza*

A new people were created during this period of time. The Spanish were the invaders, victors, colonizers, and oppressors. The indigenous people were those invaded, vanquished, colonized, and oppressed. Regardless of the bloodbath and holocaust, this resulted in a very interesting cultural twist in world history. The victor and colonizer bred and intermarried with the vanquished and colonized. This created a new race, the *mestizo*, the blending of two races—Spanish and indigenous. In Spanish, *mestizo, mezcla,* and *mestizaje* refer to the racial mixture or biological amalgamation of different races blending together. This was the creation of a new race that had never existed before in human history. The biological and cultural intermarriage of the Spanish and the indigenous people was the birth of *La Raza*.

As a result of this historical situation, today's Latinos and *Latino Americanos* are a race of *mestizos*. The exception is Latin Americans of pure Spanish heritage who have never bred with the indigenous people and indigenous people who have never mixed with the Spanish. Not only is this *mestizaje* a biological blending, but most importantly, it is a cultural fusion of indigenous and Spanish cultures. Consider the food, traditions, customs, rituals, and celebrations practiced in Latino culture. What are examples of Latino culture that originate from the Spanish European heritage and culture? What are examples of Latino culture that emanate from the indigenous cultural roots? Due to this dynamic historical process, the final and ultimate result is a Latino culture that is multiethnic, multiracial, and multicultural.

Africa's Legacy

There was another dynamic blending into the cultural blood of *La Raza*. A labor shortage occurred in the colonies. This was, in part, due to the harsh working conditions suffered by the peons. The diseases brought by the Spanish continued to plague the indigenous population. During this period, Spain imported African slaves to the Américas. According to *The Course of Mexican History* by Meyer, Sherman, and Deeds, *perhaps two hundred thousand Africans entered Mexico during the colonial period.*[3] In most cases, these Africans served as peons and worked side by side with the *indios*. In future decades, these Africans assimilated with *indios* and *mestizos* and contributed to the racial mixture of Latin América and the Caribbean. The African blood and culture eventually blended into the dynamic cultural roots of *La Raza*. The term *mulato* was used to describe this unique and distinct racial mixture. African cultural characteristics thus became an integral part of Latino culture. This was the story of Africa's legacy in México and *Latino América*.

CATHOLICISM AND THE INDIGENOUS POPULATION: THE STORY OF *LA VIRGEN DE GUADALUPE*

The indigenous population had religion and religious traditions going back many generations. This included religious philosophy, traditions, customs, rituals, and celebrations. Religious personal beliefs were strong among individuals, family, and the community. Indigenous religious philosophy believed in the Creator and the divine creation of all things. Their religion included stories of creation or how humans and all life were created. Religion meant a deep respect for the dynamic balance and equilibrium among humans, Mother Earth, and the universe. Many of the religious stories were in the form of analogies, metaphors, parables, and symbolism. Religious traditions were very strong among the indigenous population.

The Spanish imported and imposed Christianity on the New World. The Catholic Church was very powerful and influential during the time of *Nueva España*. It was a major player in government, politics, and economics. The Church was also a major landlord. The impact of Catholicism affected the daily life of the indigenous people. Since the Spanish controlled the ruling ideology, they attempted to force the indigenous population to accept Christianity. Spaniards were very ethnocentric about their religion. There was a strong cultural clash and conflict between Catholicism and the indigenous religious traditions. The indigenous people resisted, but found themselves overwhelmed by the pressure to convert. After the story of Juan Diego and *La Virgen de Guadalupe* became widespread, there was a wholesale conversion of *indios* to Catholicism. As a result of the cultural clash, the indigenous people assimilated their traditional religious beliefs with Christianity.

According to the religious Catholic tradition, in 1531, there was a poor peon *indio* by the name of Juan Diego. As he was walking through the countryside, a vision appeared. The mystical vision was a beautiful woman. She talked to him and said she was Mary, Mother of Christ. Juan was afraid and confused. The Lady in the vision told him that she wanted a church built in that very place. Juan Diego recounted the incredible story to the local bishop and was met with much skepticism. The bishop asked for proof. How could he believe such an inconceivable story? Why would the Mother of Christ appear to some unworthy Indian peon? On Diego's final encounter with her, she made rose bushes appear during that barren December winter. She asked him to pick the roses and take them to the bishop. Diego placed the beautiful roses on his *tilma* (*zarape*, a blanket-like garment) and ran to the church. When he got to the bishop, Juan Diego unrolled the *tilma,* and the roses had imprinted the image of *La Virgen de Guadalupe* on the cloth. All were awed.

This religious account of Juan Diego and *La Virgen de Guadalupe* is still a strong belief in the Catholic community after hundreds of years. Did this apparition really happen? Who knows? The Church has declared that it did. In fact, Juan Diego has been declared a saint by the Vatican in Rome. Even science has become enthralled by this controversy. In the final analysis, science cannot prove or disprove the apparition of the Virgin Mary in México. The evidence is baffling. Therefore, this religious issue is not a matter to be resolved by science. Instead, it is a matter of faith. Faith and religious belief go beyond the realm of science, the scientific method, and empiricism. This is a religious tradition that permeates the Mexican Catholic community.

Why is *La Virgen de Guadalupe* an important topic in Chicano-Latino Studies? In fact, the study of culture includes the study of religion and religious tradition. The location where the story took place is a few miles north of México City. Tens of thousands of people go to the location where the church was built, as requested by *La Virgen de Guadalupe.* Adjacent to the original church is a new, modern church called *La Basilica.* Here people view the actual cloth supposedly worn by Juan Diego with the image of *La Virgen de Guadalupe. La Virgen* has continued as a very strong religious tradition in Mexican and Mexican American culture. For instance, take the great Chicano leader, the late César Chávez. Any rally or march sponsored by Chávez and the United Farm Workers always displayed a banner with *La Virgen de Guadalupe.* From the Chicano-Latino perspective, religion is a significant aspect of culture and cultural traditions. Many people still celebrate *Día de La Virgen de Guadalupe* on December 12 of every year.

AZTLÁN DURING THE TIME OF SPANISH COLONIZATION

Aztlán is known as the legendary homeland of the Azteca-Mexica. From the perspective of the Chicano Movement, Aztlán is declared to be the Southwest of the United States. This is the expansive territory from California to Texas. Due to indigenous historical antecedents, Chicanos consider their cultural roots to be planted in Aztlán, the Southwest. (This topic will be discussed in upcoming chapters.)

From the Spanish perspective, this land was northern New Spain, *Nueva España*. The Spaniards came through and claimed the land for themselves and their mother country. Spain claimed to have discovered and founded these territories. The Spanish explorers included Alvar Núñez Cabeza de Vaca, Estéban, Eusebio Francisco Kino, Francisco Vásquez de Coronado, Juan Bautista de Anda, Juan de Oñate, Juan Rodríguez de Cabrillo, Junípero Serra, Marcos de Niza, Sebastián Vizcaíno, and many others. These Spanish were doing the work of their mother country and at the same time hoping to acquire status, prestige, and wealth. A few attained riches, many failed, and a few died trying.

The Spanish built missions throughout this territory of northern *Nueva España*. This was called the mission system. The purpose of the missions was to establish a social, cultural, and religious foundation in the territory, according to the Spaniards. The Spanish and the church priests attempted to gather and Christianize the local Indians, *indios*. The end result was an exploitation of labor and cultural genocide of indigenous life ways. The locations where the missions were established later grew into larger towns.

Note to Students   What did you learn about the missions and the mission system in elementary school? What did you learn about the famous Spanish explorers in the Southwest of the United States? What are the cities in your area that started from an old Spanish mission?

In reality, the lands were originally inhabited by indigenous people thousands of years earlier. They surveyed and established communities in habitable locations. The indigenous people lived in clusters based on what was the most habitable and ecologically friendly territory. This included beautiful lakes, rivers, foothills, forests, and pleasant valleys. The true founders of Aztlán included, for example, Apache, Comanche, Hopi, Navajo, Pueblo, Ute, Yaqui, Yokut, Zuñi, and many other cultural groups. They established the infrastructure in Aztlán that made it possible for future generations of all people to inhabit these territories. Today's indigenous people are the direct descendants of the people who founded and established communities in this land way before Spanish exploration and colonization.

THE FANTASY HERITAGE

Long, long ago the borderlands were settled by Spanish grandees and caballeros, a gentle people, accustomed to the luxurious softness of fine clothes, to well-trained servants, to all the amenities of civilized European living. . . . All in all, this life of Spain-away-from-Spain in the borderlands was very romantic, idyllic, very beautiful. . . .

In this passage from *North from Mexico* by Carey McWilliams, the concluding statement is the clincher: "Indeed, it's really a shame that it never existed."[4] Why promote the fantasy heritage of the Spanish?

This is the myth of the Spanish grandee, which has been propagated for all these years. The Spanish explorers have been glorified as epic heroes larger than life. Stories have romanticized the life and times of Spanish colonizers in the Southwest. The result has been to promote Spanish Eurocentrism and ethnocentric attitudes. With all the stories of epic adventures and romantic lifestyles, who *wouldn't* want to identify with the Spanish grandees and *caballeros*? Hollywood movies, such as *Zorro,* have been at the forefront of promoting the fantasy heritage in popular culture.

In reality, the main work settling the Southwest was done by *pobladores. Pobladores* were everyday settlers and common folk doing the legwork and the toil. They labored doing everything necessary, including building the missions, farming, and ranching. According to our friend Carey McWilliams in *North from Mexico,* the real settlement of the Southwest was accomplished by *mestizos, indios,* and *mulatos.*

The *fantasy heritage* has romanticized the Spanish explorers way beyond reality. They have received all the praise and accolades. It is a sad disservice that the fantasy heritage has served to deny the Mexican heritage in the settlement and establishment of what later became the Southwestern United States.

THE BIRTH OF MÉXICO. SIGNIFICANCE OF MEXICAN INDEPENDENCE DAY

What is the significance of the 16th of September? *El Grito de Dolores* on *dieciséis de septiembre,* 1810, by Father Miguel Hidalgo y Costilla, is commemorated by Mexicans throughout the world as the initial public manifestation for independence from three hundred years of Spanish colonial rule. Mexicans celebrate Mexican Independence Day as the start of the war of freedom from Spain. Similarly, people in the United States celebrate the Fourth of July commemorating the revolutionary war by the thirteen colonies against England.

Miguel Hidalgo y Costilla was born on May 8, 1753, in Corralejo, Guanajuato. As a *criollo,* he was educated for the priesthood, taught theology, and later became director at the College of San Nicolás in Morelia. He had several posts as a parish priest. It is said about Hidalgo that his personal life was not consistent with the church's traditional code of clerical conduct and ethics. The church was conservative and promoted the status quo; he was a liberal. Therefore, Hidalgo came under the church's scrutiny. He was very much influenced by European philosophical schools of thought relating to controversial philosophies of the time.

On September 16, 1810, Hidalgo rang the church bells early in the morning and made his famous cry for independence and freedom from Spanish rule. Known as *El Grito de Dolores*, he proclaimed the independence of México to the cry, *Long live our Lady of Guadalupe! Death to bad government! Death to the Gachupines!* With the help of his fellow revolutionaries such as Ignacio Allende, Hidalgo's call ignited the tinder of native resentment against Spanish excesses and exploitation. This rallying cry resulted in an explosion of flaming revolution. Hidalgo led the movement toward the independence of México from Spain. The banner of *La Virgen de Guadalupe* served as the symbol of the movement for freedom.

Miguel Hidalgo won several battles and was finally captured, executed, and decapitated. The war continued with leaders such as José María Morelos y Pavón, a mestizo. After his capture and execution, the war persisted with other famous revolutionaries such as Vicente Guerrero, Guadalupe Victoria, and many others. *Criollos, mestizos,* and *indios* continued to fight against the Spanish crown. The period of Mexican independence lasted from 1810 to 1821. During this time, much of the strife revolved around the power of the government, the military, and the church. Remember the previous discussion of the *peones* and the rich and wealthy landlords. Unfortunately these unresolved questions haunted México for many years to come.

__Note to Students__   The following Mexican Independence Day, view Spanish-speaking television on the evening of September 15. It is tradition that the president of México will conduct a

© Micha Rosenwirth, 2013. Used under license from Shutterstock, Inc.

ceremony on the balcony of the National Palace, *El Palacio Nacional,* in México City. This is located at *El Zócalo,* which is the plaza in the historical center of México City. At this time, the president recognizes the heroic role of Miguel Hidalgo and recites his cry for independence. *¡Viva México!*

Note to Students   Reading and Research. *Battle of Medina.* The Movement for México's independence from Spain also occurred in the Northern Territories. Do research on the Battle of Medina and the *Tejano* declaration of independence from Spain in 1813. Brave and courageous *Tejanos* organized and mobilized their forces against Spanish colonization and oppression.

MÉXICO, THE BIRTH OF A NEW COUNTRY: BEWARE OF YOUR NEIGHBOR WHO WANTS SOMETHING YOU'VE GOT!

¡Viva México! The birth of a new country! Unfortunately, México was born a new country politically and economically bankrupt from three hundred years of colonial rule and Spanish exploitation. It was a very difficult birth. Classes of poor and privileged were pitted against each other. Crisis after crisis plagued the new country. Internal strife between political factions was the norm. And if this was not enough internal crises, lurking in the dark chapters of world history was an aggressive neighbor manifesting a destiny that would compound disaster for México. Looming in the future was a war where México would lose the northern territories, along with the Mexicans who had settled that land. The Mexican-American War, 1846–1848, is the story of the first Mexicans who became part of the United States. In the war, not only did the United States acquire a huge territory from México but also a population of *Mexicanos.* The story of Aztlán and *La Raza* continues.

CHAPTER DISCUSSION QUESTIONS

1. What was the purpose of the conquest by the Spanish?
2. Discuss and explain the results and consequences of the Spanish conquest.
3. What is the meaning of *la conquista* for Mexican Americans and Latinos today?
4. What is colonization? What does it mean to be conquered and colonized?
5. How does Christianity, specifically Catholicism, relate to Latinos today?
6. México and the other countries of *Latino América* were colonized by Spain for three hundred years. What does this mean in terms of Mexican American and Latino culture today?

7. What is the *fantasy heritage*? Why do you think the Spanish explorers have been glorified and romanticized? Why do you think Mexicans are not given credit and recognition for their contribution in the founding and establishment of the Southwest?

© Betacam-SP/Shutterstock.com

CHAPTER 4

THE MEXICAN-AMERICAN WAR, 1846–1848
LEGACY OF CONFLICT: U.S. CONQUEST OF MÉXICO

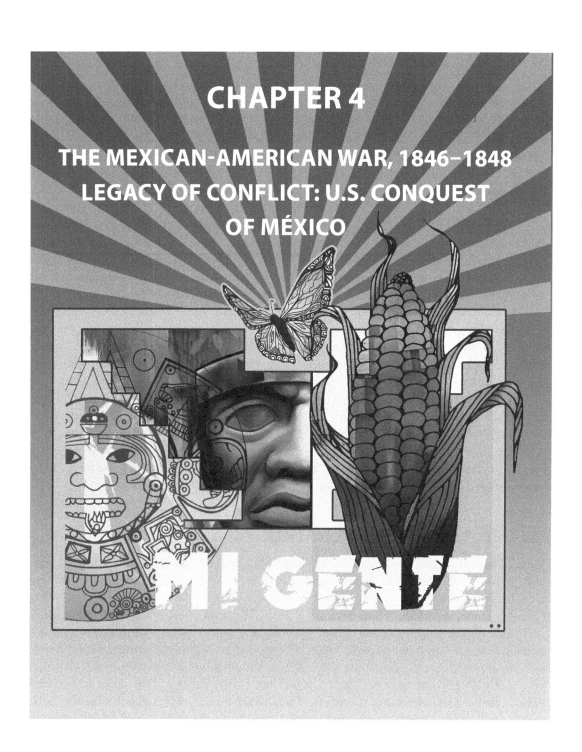

SPAIN AND COLONIAL MÉXICO

What were the results and consequences of 300 years of Spain's colonial domination over the Américas? México's war of independence did not resolve the many internal conflicts and contradictions that were inherent to the process of colonization. Yes, for the Spanish *hacendados* and landlords it was a time of prosperity and wealth. Across the Atlantic Ocean, Spain's royalty bathed in the riches arriving from the New World. Spanish colonization was based on the exploitation of human labor in the most extreme form and under harsh conditions. Living in social and cultural bondage, the poor working class was at the mercy of Spanish society. For working families, anything could happen and almost everything did. Imagine the worst, including child labor. The Spanish controlled the land, economics, politics, government, the church, and the military. How functional can a society be when the social structures are based on the oppression of the lower class of *peones*, or peons? This peonage system was destined to implode and explode. The system's internal contradictions and the schism between the rich and the poor would eventually cause Spanish society to unravel.

As was previously discussed, the territory of *Nueva España* was massive. However, boundary changes occurred that had ramifications and economic, political, and international implications for future generations. In 1800, Spain ceded a huge territory to France. In 1803, France sold it to the United States. This is known as the Louisiana Purchase. In the future, this becomes the Midwest of the United States. In 1819, Spain ceded Florida to the United States in the Adams-Onis Treaty (Transcontinental Treaty). The intent of the treaty was to settle the boundary of the two counties. This defined the western border of the United States at the mouth of the Sabine River. Today this is the boundary between Louisiana and Texas. These boundary changes affected Spanish exploration and colonization in the New World. After Mexican independence from Spain, 1821, the Adams-Onis Treaty would have implications for the border dispute between México and the United States.

MÉXICO: THE BIRTH OF A NATION

México's independence movement started in 1810, a time of prolonged social unrest struggling to resolve the many social and cultural contradictions under Spanish domination. This included defining the role and power of the government, the military, and the church. Subsequently, the nation of México was declared in 1821. This new country was born economically and politically bankrupt as a result of over 300 years of Spanish colonization. Stability was questionable. México had much experience with kings, queens, monarchies, and Spanish royalty but little experience with democracy and self-rule. The evolution and development of México's personality, or Mexican national character, was not clearly defined. This social and cultural developmental process was slow to emerge. It would take time, experience, and maturity for the country to develop a Mexican national consciousness and sense of national unity. Patriotism proliferates when the people feel a strong sense of unity, pride, and national character.

U.S. WESTWARD EXPANSION AND THE STORY OF THE MEXICAN-AMERICAN WAR, 1846–1848

A long chain of events resulted in a war that had reverberations for decades to come. The story begins with the migration into the Mexican territory of *Tejas* by American settlers or colonists. This was the pattern of westward expansion by the United States. These colonists started calling the territory Texas and themselves Texans (or Texians). The original Mexican settlers of this territory called themselves *Tejanos*.

As discussed above, the Adams-Onis Treaty, 1819, dealt with the issue of borders and boundaries. As part of the treaty negotiations, the United States renounced claims to *Tejas*, recognizing the territory as part of the Mexican state of Coahuila. Some Americans opposed and disagreed with the provisions of the Adams-Onis Treaty, claiming that the Louisiana Purchase included the Mexican territory of *Tejas* all the way to the *Río Grande*.

The Long Expedition, 1819

A case in point was the questionable acts of James Long. He renounced the Adams-Onis Treaty. In 1819, the so-called Long Expedition to Texas attempted to establish the Republic of Texas, and his followers proclaimed him president. This attempt was aborted and short lived. In his second expedition, Long brought in some 300 troops. Later he was captured by Spanish authorities, imprisoned, and shot a few months later in 1822. Imagine his audacity and insistence that Texas was an American possession! What was James Long thinking? Was it territorial acquisition, westward expansion, or personal aggrandizement, or all of these? Apparently he was willing to fight and die for his beliefs as a matter of principle.

Initial American Colonists to México

After Mexican independence in 1821, México opened *Tejas* to some American settlements. In 1821, México gave Stephen Austin permission to settle in *Tejas*. Previously Spain had given his father, Moses Austin, such permission. That year, he founded the colony called San Félipe de Austin. The initial colonists agreed to obey all Mexican laws, change their religion to Catholicism, and take an oath of allegiance to the Mexican republic. As immigrants and newcomers, this was only to be expected. Americans soon became resentful and rebellious toward México. Mexican authorities became alarmed with the large number of immigrants crossing the border into México. The flood of illegal immigrants into *Tejas* would soon be out of control.

In 1824, President John Quincy Adams offered México $1 million for Texas. México refused the offer, and Adams prepared an aggressive diplomatic maneuver to manipulate the situation. The tension increased between the two countries.

Joel Poinsett, 1825, Minister to México

In 1825 President John Quincy Adams sent Joel Poinsett to México City. Poinsett was charged with influencing México to sell some of its land. Mexican politicians saw Poinsett as interfering in internal affairs and equated the name Poinsett with political treachery. The term *poinsettismo* was coined to describe his meddling and intrusive conduct.

The Republic of Fredonia, 1826

Another U.S. colonist leader was Hayden Edwards, an American land speculator. In 1826, Edwards and his men invaded *Nacogdoches* (located in east *Tejas)* in the Fredonia Rebellion. He declared independence from México and the *Republic of Fredonia.* Mexican authorities immediately squashed this revolt and rebellion. From the perspective of México, this was an act of sedition. From the perspective of the United States, Americans referred to Edwards as an *apostle of democracy.* These opposing viewpoints set the stage for future conflict and war.

Opposing Viewpoints

First México passed the Decree of 1829 to abolish slavery in *Tejas.* Then México passed the Law of 1830 to prohibit further American immigration into Mexican territory. Colonists were furious. American settlers resented these laws and considered the Mexican government oppressive tyrants. President Andrew Jackson increased the conflict by offering to buy the Mexican territory of *Tejas* for up to $5 million.

In 1829, President Andrew Jackson appointed Anthony Butler to be in charge of U.S. affairs in México City. Some of his contemporaries considered him of questionable character. Supposedly, Butler attempted to bribe a Mexican official some $200,000 to "play ball" on the issue of American interests in Texas. Butler remained in México City until 1836, reporting to Jackson on México's intentions regarding Texas.

By 1830, there were approximately 20,000 American colonists in the Mexican territory of *Tejas.* They brought in some 2,000 slaves from the United States to do slave labor on cotton plantations. Americans continued streaming into Mexican territory.

The difference of opinion was clear, that is, opposing viewpoints on the situation. Americans felt anger and hostility and viewed México as an obstacle to U.S. progress. Americans saw themselves as fighting for freedom, liberty, and the right to settle. Mexicans were alarmed by the massive immigration of *illegal aliens* invading their territory with intent to organize a revolution. This intent was made clear with the actions of Sam Houston and the *War Party* in 1831. The purpose of the war party was to organize and mobilize an independence movement against México by any and all means possible. This would be the precursor to the consolidation of Texas into the United States. By 1832, a total state of insurrection existed in *Tejas,* meaning that the Americans were in total rebellion against México. The Mexican government saw the Texans' actions as overt acts of sedition. To México it was a plot and conspiracy to invade and occupy Mexican territory.

Powerful land companies were constantly influencing American politics. There was constant lobbying by these companies in Washington, DC, to protect and secure American interests in Texas. This included the Galveston Bay and the Texas Land Company of New York. American's strong lobbying campaign in 1834 greatly strained relations between the United States and México.

Massive immigration continued into Texas spurred on by leaders such as Stephen Austin. The colonists contemplated a take-over of Texas by their sheer numbers. Americans forged an economic union with the United States starting with the cotton industry. The colonists established trade and commerce with the United States. Their objective was to Americanize Texas, break away from México and join the American union. By 1835 there were about 30,000 American colonists to a population of only about 5,000 Mexicans living in Texas. The massive encroachment by American colonists into Mexican territory set the stage for the Texas revolution against México.

The Alamo, 1836, and the Texas Revolution

At this point General Antonio López de Santa Anna, a very controversial figure in Mexican history, enters the picture. In 1835, Santa Anna marched some 1,400 troops up to *Tejas*, arriving near San Antonio in February 1836. Many of his troops were conscripts. Overall, they were ill equipped, ill prepared, uneducated, and poorly trained. Some of these draftees were *Indios*, who did not even speak Spanish. Santa Anna was on a mission to take back control of the Mexican territory of *Tejas*.

Upon hearing of Santa Anna's arrival, the Texans decided to make a stand against México. The leaders organized a defense of San Antonio and barricaded themselves in the old Spanish mission known as the Alamo (a former Franciscan mission; San Antonio de Valero, 1718). There were about 187 inside the Alamo. Their leaders included William Barret Travis, James "Jim" Bowie, Davey Crockett, James Butler Bonham, and others. On the morning of February 23, 1836, General Santa Anna led an attack against the Alamo. The battle of the Alamo was a 13-day siege ending March 6. A few surrendered (7?), including Davey Crockett, and were later executed. The Alamo legend has it that they all died in battle. A few *Tejanos* who sided with the Texans also died inside the Alamo. Santa Anna did not foresee that the death of these Texans would result in even more fervor and support from American politicians in the United States.

The Historic Battle of the Alamo and the Myth of the Alamo

A visit to the Alamo today clearly illustrates the legacy of the Alamo in terms of opposing viewpoints discussed above. Walking into the Alamo, visitors are in awe as they see the images of these great men who were *freedom fighters*. In Texas history, those who died at the

Alamo are *great American heroes*. A visitor brochure states something like: *Thus stands The Alamo. A shrine to courage and the struggle for liberty. A symbol for eternity that free men will stand and die for their ideals.* In the State of Texas this is a historical landmark, shrine, and considered hallowed ground. It is a shrine dedicated to the brave courageous men who struggled for freedom, independence, and the Republic of Texas. From this perspective, they were freedom-loving Texas defenders. They are legendary folk heroes to many Americans.

As an opposing viewpoint, some American historians question the motivation and intention of these so-called *freedom fighters* within the context of the entire movement for westward expansion. Yes, Americans fought and died at the Alamo. And they have been elevated to greatness and put on a pedestal for Americans to admire. However, it behooves the student of American history to see issues from a multiplicity of perspectives including opposing viewpoints. For example, take Jim Bowie and Davey Crockett. At the time they were considered great frontiersmen, Indian fighters, and brave adventurers. This was a time in history of the American West when Indians were killed at will and sometimes for sport. Jim Bowie was a slave trader and land speculator. Davey Crockett was known as *King of the Wild Frontier*. According to Alamo myth, he *fought like a tiger,* killing Mexicans with his bare hands. Frontiersmen would get paid for killing Indians and be paid a bounty for their scalps. Unfortunately, many Americans learned American history by watching television and movies. This includes the 1950s TV series *Davey Crockett*. Reruns are still aired today. Also, very popular was the 1960 movie, *The Alamo*, staring John Wayne. Since the Wayne movie, Hollywood has produced a number of remakes using the same paradigm portraying the epic battle of freedom fighting heroes struggling for democracy and self-determination.

Remember the Alamo! An interesting and controversial story was published in the *New York Times* entitled "New Times, A New Look at Those Alamo Stories."[1] Texas prides itself on its historical struggle to establish the *Lone Star Republic*. However, a generation of new writers, researchers, historians, and politicians rebuke and challenge epic stories of the so-called *Texas defenders*. These new writers call the Alamo leaders "nuts, scoundrels . . . Anglo land-grabbers." A few interesting and controversial examples regarding Alamo leaders include the following: Commander William Barret Travis, "crazed from drinking mercury to treat venereal disease." General Sam Houston, "a girdle-wearing opium addict." Jim Bowie, "stole a hoard of silver and gold from Apaches he had butchered." It may be that the story of the Alamo has become more myth than historical reality and "the latest generation of writers has challenged its very significance. For them, the Alamo symbolizes not the American settlers' struggle against tyranny but U.S. imperialism and racism triumphant over Mexicans and Indians". So much for, Remember the Alamo!

Note to Students This *New York Times* story represents an alternative historical paradigm to that of the *freedom fighters, defenders of Texas,* and the epic struggle of the *Texas Revolution*. Remember that much of history is a matter of interpretation and perspective. Regardless of myth or reality, a society promotes its prevailing paradigms and dominant ideology.

This is transformed into people's attitude, behavior, values, and beliefs. For the entire news story, please see Endnotes and Google reference information to see the original news report.

March 1836: Battle of Coleto Creek and the Goliad Massacre

There were contentious Texans on the war path against Mexican troops throughout the area. After the Battle of Coleto, the rebellious Texans were taken captive by the Mexican army in the town of Goliad. The prisoners were executed along with their commander James Fannin. Getting word of the executions, the Texans were furious. They considered the executions a *massacre*. So the battle cry for revenge against México was not only *Remember the Alamo* but now also *Remember Goliad*. Texans felt contemptuous toward the Mexican government.

April 21, 1836: Battle of San Jacinto. Treaty of Velasco

Apparently Santa Anna was confident after his recent victories, including skirmishes with General Sam Houston. Houston outmaneuvered Santa Anna in a battle that lasted less than half an hour. Houston organized a swift assault and his army attacked with the rallying cry of *Remember the Alamo! Remember Goliad!* Some 630 Mexican soldiers were killed and 9 Texans died. Under duress, Santa Anna signed the Treaty of Velasco giving away *Tejas*. The Mexican government never recognized nor ratified the treaty. Santa Anna did not have the authority under the Mexican Constitution to negotiate any treaty agreements. Here again opposing viewpoints and the point of contention surface. From the perspective of Texans, they were now independent since Santa Anna signed the Treaty of Velasco. From the Mexican perspective, *Tejas* remained a territory of México, even if out of control. In this same year, Sam Houston was elected president of the Republic of Texas, and the new republic was officially recognized by the United States. A few years later, in 1845, Texas was annexed by the United States. México was irate but to no avail.

The Slidell Mission

In November, 1845, President James K. Polk (of Tennessee) sent John Slidell to México City. Slidell was authorized to offer up to $50 million dollars for México's vast northern territories, including Nuevo México and Alta California. The Mexican government was not interested in selling the land. México was in fact insulted with Slidell's persistence and rejected him. Since México refused to sell, Polk would soon turn to a military option. Slidell recommended that México be *chastised*.

THE MEXICAN-AMERICAN WAR, 1846–1848: INVASION OF MÉXICO

In the United States political debate over relations with México was the hot topic of the day as pressure mounted over hotly contested issues. In 1845, President James K. Polk was actively maneuvering American politics in preparation for war. He was well aware that México was incensed because the United States annexed Texas as a state. Polk kept in constant contact with Thomas Larkin, American consul to *Alta California*. His agenda was a strategy of preparedness in case war was declared by either country. In 1845–1846 John C. Fremont, an American military officer and explorer, was playing the so-called *Texas Game* in *Alta California*. He was agitating for American colonists to revolt against Mexican authorities. Subsequently, this resulted in the *Bear Flag Revolt* by American colonists in that territory. This sort of activity coincided with Polk's political agenda.

A key factor leading up to the war was the border dispute between the United States and México. According to Polk, the southern boundary of Texas was the *Río Grande* (located today in southern Texas, as the boundary between the two countries). According to México, the southern boundary of *Tejas* was 150 miles north of the *Río Grande* at the *Nueces* River (located today near Corpus Christi in southeastern Texas).

In July 1845, Polk sent General Zachary Taylor to Texas, and in 1846, he ordered General Zachary Taylor to the *Nueces* River. President Santa Anna sent his troops to the *Río Grande*. The first skirmish occurred where American soldiers were killed. When the news arrived in Washington, President Polk's message to congress was that, México has passed the boundary of the United States, has invaded *our* territory, and shed American blood upon American soil. He therefore called for Congress to declare war against México. The war commenced.

The United States waged war on several fronts. In California (then called *Alta California*) the American forces rallied under Army Captain John C. Fremont, Commodore Robert Stockton, Commodore John Drake Sloat, General W. Stephen Kearny, and others and took control of the major cities including San Francisco, Sonoma, Sacramento, and Los Angeles. Commodore Sloat occupied the state capital, Monterey, on July 7, 1846, and raised the American flag.

The first Mexican settlers in México's territory known as Alta California called themselves *Californios*. The *Californios* managed several victories against the invaders. Near Los Angeles, an organized group of *rancheros* and *vaqueros* armed with lancers defeated American troops led by U.S. Navy Captain William Mervine. This was the *Battle of Dominguez Rancho*. In the *Battle of San Pasqual*, *Californios* with lancers defeated the troops of General Kearny near San Diego. The Treaty of Cahuenga, written both in English and Spanish, was signed on January 13, 1847. It was an informal agreement that brought the open warfare to an end.

On another war front, General Zachary Taylor and his troops crossed the *Río Grande* and moved south. He captured major cities such as Matamoros, Camargo, Monterrey, Saltillo, and others. His greatest victory was the Battle of Buena Vista. In the future, Taylor's victories would promote his political career in American politics.

Deep in México, Veracruz was another major war front. On the coast of the Gulf of México, the military invaders arrived in Veracruz under General Winfield Scott. He bombed the city into submission with heavy barrage of artillery. Men, women, and children ran for their lives. The siege of Veracruz lasted a dozen long days. The U.S. amphibious landing laid waste to the city.

From Veracruz, the U.S. military campaign moved west to México City. General Santa Anna made an incompetent attempt to stop Scott's troops. His failure resulted in a bloodbath for his army. The final defense of México City was the Battle of Chapultepec. The Mexican troops were few and severely ill-prepared for this assault. With the fall of Chapultepec Castle, General Scott was in charge of the military occupation of México City. As word got to the United States, General Winfield Scott became an American national hero.

Note to Students   See Glossary: *Los Niños Héroes*. See also: Saint Patrick's Battalion.

All Is Fair in Love and War

It is said that President Porfirio Díaz once lamented, "Poor México, so far from God and so close to the United States." It is interesting to do a review of literature on the Mexican-American War. One of the most obvious omissions in the literature is a lack of discussion regarding war crimes and atrocities committed by American soldiers attacking México. A significant number of U.S. troops were volunteers and not professionally trained soldiers. At times they attacked to the revengeful cry of *Remember the Alamo!* and *Remember Goliad!* killing innocent men, women, and children. There are writers who are apologists for the war, merely saying that it was a *bad war* in a time when the United States was going through conflict and economic and political change. This explanation absolves the United States from the responsibility of questionable mean-spirited, aggressive, and negative behavior during the war. The most popular apologist was American writer Justin Harvey Smith, during the early 1900s. He actually claimed that México was at fault and responsible for the war. Fortunately, his ethnocentric perspective is discounted by honest historians today. The reality is that in this war, the United States was on the offensive as the aggressor and México on the defense, attempting to protect Mexican territory. Also, an analysis of the Texas Revolution is incomplete without dealing with the issue of slavery. How can a society that purports to believe in freedom and democracy rationalize the institution of slavery as a way of life? The slavery question returned later to haunt the United States in the form of the American Civil War. The Mexican-American War, was in fact, a crisis for American democracy. *All is fair in love and war . . .* Really?

CRITICAL PERSPECTIVES, DISCUSSION, AND DEBATE: LEGACY OF CONFLICT, U.S. CONQUEST OF MÉXICO

In order to fully understand the social and cultural status of Mexican Americans in today's society, it is necessary to consider historical perspectives. This includes an analysis of the ethnic and racial relations between Mexican Americans and the dominant American society. The roots of this conflict go back to the era when northern México was annexed by conquest.

Glenn W. Price, author of *Origins of the War with Mexico, the Polk-Stockton Intrigue* states, "America was . . . a racist society."[2] This statement is quite an indictment open to debate and discussion. When racism takes root in a society, it becomes tightly interwoven into the very infrastructure of society. Institutionalized racism, then, is social and cultural oppression at the highest level. Mexican Americans were forced to navigate and survive generations of social and cultural conflict.

There were voices against the war but these people were in the minority. Here are three examples. Congressman Abraham Lincoln of Illinois argued against President Polk with the *Spot Resolution*. Lincoln challenged the president to show the *spot*, referring to the location where Polk claimed that American blood was shed on American soil. Congressman Lincoln went on to say that the war had been unnecessarily and unconstitutionally started by Polk when he sent American troops to the *Nueces River*. Lincoln called Polk's argument *sheerest deception*.[3] Another example was Senator Alexander Stephens of Georgia. (A few years later Stephens became Vice President of the Confederacy.) Senator Stephens coined the famous phrase, *Polk the Mendacious* adding that the President Polk was a man whom none could believe.[4] A third example was the famous American author, Henry David Thoreau. Thoreau failed to pay his taxes as an act of opposition to the Mexican-American War, which he considered an unjust war. During his stay in jail, he wrote his famous essay, "Civil Disobedience." Thoreau denounces the unjust war against Mexico and speaks to the issue of government law, which, though it may have been enacted with the consent of the majority, is nonetheless in conflict with moral law.[5] These are only a few examples of a small but vocal minority against the Mexican-American War.

The war between the United States and México was the genesis of the Mexican American or *Chicano*. Before the war, the people living in northern México were Mexican. After the war, they found themselves living in a different country. Thus the concept of, *We didn't cross the border, the border crossed us*. This situation marks the start of a people's oppression as second-class citizens and *strangers in their own land*.

What were the prevailing paradigms or dominant thought among influential Americans? Glenn W. Price goes on to illustrate that during the period of the Mexican-American War:

> *The diplomacy of the United States with Mexico reflected the prevailing judgment of the American people on Mexicans. The attitude was that there was very little difference between an Indian and a Mexican ("the only good Indian is a dead Indian"); serious and respectful diplomacy was out of place in either case. By the time of the Mexican War, it was standard political rhetoric that the Mexicans were incapable of self-government; the argument turned on whether or not the United States should undertake to govern them. One argument ran that it would be a violation of American political principle to rule them as colonials, and it would be destructive of the American government to allow the Mexicans to participate in governing. The other position, as put by the*

chairman of the Senate Committee on Foreign relations in 1848, was that the Mexicans could be removed to reservations just as the Indians in the United States had been, and as for voting, "the Indians had not gone up to vote that he knew of."[6]

The attitudes and prevailing paradigms of the 1800s are quite revealing. According to the American belief and philosophy of *manifest destiny*, the United States had the God-given right to spread its sacred institutions from ocean to ocean. This concept was coined by an influential journalist, John L. O'Sullivan.

Undoubtedly, American economic and political interests were instrumental in initializing a war in which México lost over half the land, including 1,300 miles of coast on the Pacific. Commercial expansionists could forsee the wealth and power that could belong to the United States merely for the taking. According to *Empire of the Pacific* by Norman A. Graebner:

For American expansion to the Pacific was a precise and calculated movement . . . . Any interpretation of westward extension beyond Texas is meaningless unless defined in terms of commerce and harbors."[7]

This reason for the U.S. to go to war against México is called Maritime Destiny. In fact, the Mexican-American war was only the climax in a long process whereby the United States had tried for years to obtain Mexican territory all the way to the Pacific Ocean.

Nicholas P. Trist was sent to Mexico by President Polk to negotiate a treaty. The war came to an end with the Treaty of Guadalupe Hidalgo, ratified by México, February 2, 1848. It seems that Polk was furious with Trist. Here was the opportunity for the U.S. to obtain even more Mexican territory. The president was very disappointed with Trist and the territorial agreement.

The rights and privileges that belong to Mexicans can be deduced from the Treaty of Guadalupe Hidalgo and from the accompanying Protocol. According to historian Feliciano Rivera:

"The so-called Protocol of Queretaro was merely a document resulting from the conversations of the American and Mexican ministers who were to exchange the ratifications. . . . The Protocol was an effort to assure the Mexican government that the rights of the Mexicans in the territory ceded to the United States would be protected.

Furthermore, according to the Treaty, Mexicans in the ceded territory shall be:

admitted as soon as possible, according to the principles of the Federal Constitution, to the enjoyment of all the rights of citizens of the United States. In the mean time, they shall be maintained and protected in the enjoyment of their liberty, their property, and the civil rights now vested in them according to the Mexican laws. With respect to political rights, their condition shall be on equality with that of the inhabitants of the other territories of the United States. . . ."[8]

These rights and privileges were implicit and explicit.

Violations of the social and cultural rights of Mexicans are more the rule than the exception. The Treaty of Guadalupe Hidalgo has not been upheld despite the fact that Article VI of the U.S. Constitution states that: *"all Treaties made, or which shall be made, under the authority of the United States, shall be the supreme law of the land, and the Judges in every state shall be bound thereby. . . .* One of the greatest violations of these rights has been the state governments. The California Constitutional Convention of 1879 was a typical example. A coalition of land owners and labor unions prohibited the reading of the Spanish language in the public schools. The argument was that Spanish was too foreign. In 1894, English was a requirement for voting, thereby disenfranchising the Spanish-speaking."[9]

The issue of land title serves as another example. Even though property was supposedly safeguarded in the Treaty, in reality Mexicans were coerced from their land by squatters, sharp lawyers, and corrupt land officials. Therefore, within a few years after the ratification of the Treaty, the basis of land ownership in California had drastically changed, that is, from Mexican to White American.[10] The loss of land occurred to Mexicans throughout the territory that became the Southwest of the United States.

The story of Mexican Americans saturated with violence and injustice even lasted into the 1900s. The early rancho wars between the sheep owners and the cattlemen, the wholesale lynching, and the vigilante committees are only a few examples of the violence inflicted upon Mexicans who became strangers in their own land. In an editorial dated November 18, 1922, the *New York Times* said. "the killing of Mexicans without provocation is so common as to pass almost unnoticed." In an article in *World's Work,* George Marvin reported that:

> *the killings of Mexicans . . . throughout the border in these last four years is almost incredible. . . . Some rangers have degenerated into common man-killers. There is no penalty for killing, for no jury along the border would ever convict a white man for shooting a Mexican . . . . Reading over the Secret Service records makes you feel almost as though there were an open game season on Mexicans along the border.[11]*

The implications of the Mexican-American War are many. For years after, the Mexican people remaining in the United States were known in México as *our brothers that were sold*. It must be remembered that Mexican Americans are the only American cultural group (besides Native American Indians) who have been annexed by conquest and the only group (again besides Native American Indians) whose rights are specifically safeguarded by Treaty provision.[12] Even though the Treaty of Guadalupe Hidalgo ended the war, repercussions have lasted to this day. The Treaty, in reality, could not provide for the integration of the Mexican culture into American society. Even though the United States was ecstatic acquiring over half of México's territory, it was not willing or prepared to assimilate a people with a different language and culture. This social and cultural conflict had far-reaching implications.

See Chapter 5 to learn about the life and culture of Mexicans in Aztlán before and after the Mexican-American War, 1846–1848. The dynamics of Mexican-American history, heritage, and culture is the result of all these historical antecedents. The saga continues in the evolution of a people. The story of Mexican Americans *is* an American epic. This *is* American history.

Note to Students   Consider the following intriguing movies related to this chapter:

The movie *Seguin* is based on the book *The Memoirs of Juan Seguin*. This movie is a dramatization of Juan Seguin and the other families who were the original settlers of the Mexican territory known as *Tejas*. *Seguin* (1982) was the first film to air on *American Playhouse* about the Latino experience. It was written and directed by Jesús Salvador Treviño.

The movie *One Man's Hero* (1999) is based on a true story. It is a moving account of the Irish who deserted the U.S. military and fought on the side of México. This is the epic story of the brave and courageous *San Patricios* (stars: Tom Berenger, Joaquim De Almeida, Daniela Romo).

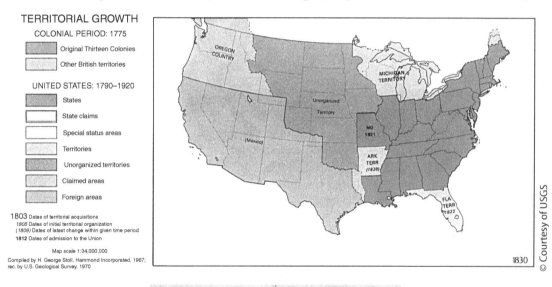

The Mexican-American War, 1846–1848 Legacy of Conflict: U.S. Conquest of México   **55**

READING AND RESEARCH

- Learn about Dos Amades. This is the story of a brave and courageous Mexican woman who led a company of lancers. Dos Amades swore not to surrender until she drove out what she called the *Northern Barbarians* from México.

- Learn about María Josefa Zozaya. She died in the Battle of Monterrey, México, while nursing wounded soldiers. María died in the battlefield and became known as the *Maid of Monterrey* for her kindness and compassion.

CHAPTER DISCUSSION QUESTIONS

1. Social science investigates issues using the scientific method of cause and effect. With this approach in mind, answer the following questions: What were the various causes of the Mexican-American War? What were the results and consequences of the Mexican-American War? Define and explain. Who? What? Where? When? Why? How?

2. What is the Treaty of Guadalupe Hidalgo? Do you believe the Treaty is a living document today? Define and explain.

3. How does the Mexican-American War, 1846–1848, relate to Mexicans and Mexican Americans today?

4. As a result of the war, the United States obtained more than half of México's territory. This is over a half-million square miles. The United States obtained clear title to Texas and all the land to California including what later became New México, Arizona, Nevada, Utah, and Colorado. What does all this mean for Mexican Americans today?

© Betacam-SP/Shutterstock.com

CHAPTER 5

THE EARLY AND LATE 1800s:
LIFE AND CULTURE OF MEXICANS
BEFORE AND AFTER THE WAR

EARLY 1800s: *MEXICANOS* IN AZTLÁN BEFORE THE MEXICAN-AMERICAN WAR, 1846–1848

In the far remote stretches of northern México, *Mexicanos* lived in their own society. These lands were not states of México but territories. Mexicans had strong cultural roots established since the days of *Nueva España*. There existed regional differences among these *Mexicanos* based on the specific location they established. In California, the Mexicans called themselves *Californios,* in New México *Nuevo Mexicanos,* and in Texas, *Tejanos*. The Mexicans were independent and autonomous thinkers philosophically and in everyday practical matters. They wanted to be in control of their lives in terms of the economy, politics, and government. For them, the capitol of México City was far, far away! *Mexicanos* in their own respective colonies developed viable cultural roots and a strong sense of cultural identity that has lasted to this day.

Note to Students   Cultural Research. Identify and interview Mexicans from your local community whose families are from California, New México, Texas, Arizona, Nevada, and Colorado. Can you identify the strong cultural identity of these *Mexicanos* from different regions?

The life of Mexicans revolved around small farming and ranching. Ranchers, *rancheros,* raised and worked with horses, cattle, and other farm animals. *Mexicanos* innovated forms of irrigation that were suitable for this unique geography and topography. *Mexicanos* established the patterns for land and water use in these territories. Over the generations, their resourcefulness was the key in adapting to the physical environment that the land had to offer. Their daily life revolved around an agricultural livelihood. Farming and ranching were the lifeblood of *Mexicano* culture during this period of rural Mexican society. Traditions, food, music, and folklore reflected life in the *ranchos* (ranches).

Note to Students   Have you traveled in today's Southwest? Notice the wide, diverse variety of topography ranging from deserts, plains, mountains, forests, and valleys. Imagine life in Aztlán during the 1800s before the Industrial Revolution! Notice the old mission style form of architecture that can still be seen in the Southwest today.

The Great American Cowboy, an American Institution

It is interesting to consider the roots of *country and western style* and tradition in the United States. People think of nothing more American than the *American cowboy*. This cowboy has evolved into a traditional icon of American popular culture. As an example, Hollywood and the mass media have perpetuated the John Wayne image of the strong and mighty cowboy during *the good old western days*. In reality, the American cowboy is a copy and rendition of the *vaquero,* meaning Mexican cowboy. The origin of the *vaquero* goes back to the time of *Nueva España*. The Spanish brought horses and cattle into the New World. Mexicans had three hundred years to become the best horse riders that this part of the world had ever seen. *Mexicanos* became experts at working with horses and cattle. *Vaqueros* learned the art of cattle drives and feeding livestock on fertile grazing lands. These *vaqueros* invented and innovated many of the tools and equipment that subsequently were borrowed and adapted by the American cowboy. The very language of the *Old West* is Mexican in origin, starting with concepts like *rodeo* and *lasso*. Thus, this Mexican *vaquero* established the cultural infrastructure of the Southwest. The subsequent land development by the United States was made possible due to the foundation set by these Mexicans. Foreign immigrants from the United States were not forced to reinvent the wheel thanks to the genius and ingenuity of the *vaquero* and other Mexican settlers, *pobladores*.

The Indigenous Cultures in Aztlán

Scattered throughout Aztlán also lived a number of indigenous cultures. These included Apache, Comanche, Hopi, Navajo, Pueblo, Ute, Yaqui, Yokut, Zuñi, and many, many others. Indigenous people lived here for thousands of years. The policy of Spain and México regarding the indigenous people was both benevolent and malevolent. Over the decades and centuries, the Spanish and the Mexicans had a mixed reaction toward the native indigenous people of Aztlán. On the one hand, there was genocide, oppression, and exploitation. On the other, there were intermarriages and biological blending of sorts. Resentment toward Spain and México for their deadly policies resulted in a hemorrhaging wound lasting indefinitely.

Historically, the indigenous people were native to this land, and they are still here today. The life and culture of Native American Indian people is wide and varied based on many social and cultural factors. Some live on reservations and others have assimilated into the mainstream of American society. A few tribes have created an innovative economic survival strategy of organizing Indian gaming casinos. From the perspective of the American Indian Movement, Indian people are sovereign nations with the right to maintain their freedom and autonomy. From this perspective, their aim is not to assimilate into the cultural mainstream of the United States. Their aim is to empower themselves and perpetuate indigenous history, heritage, and culture. Preserving the rich traditional Indian ways has been a very difficult struggle under the U.S. government. It is sad to say that ignorance and racism toward the indigenous people is still a crucial issue today in Aztlán.

Note to Students   Compare and contrast the cultural life of the indigenous people in the United States with *la gente indígena* in *México* and *Latino América*.

LATE 1800s: *MEXICANOS* IN AZTLÁN AFTER THE MEXICAN-AMERICAN WAR, 1846–1848

In Chicano-Latino Studies, an understanding of the Mexican-American War is pivotal in Mexican and Mexican American history, heritage, and culture. The Mexican-American War is the story that tells the way in which *Mexicanos* first became part of the United States of America. In other words, before the war, the inhabitants were *Mexicanos* living in México, and afterward they found themselves in another country, the United States. This turned out to be a major shift in the social and cultural life of Mexicans.

From the perspective of the Chicano Movement, Aztlán was the legendary homeland of the Azteca-Mexica. As a result of the Mexican-American War, the United States acquired Aztlán. The United States acquired a huge territory that became the Southwest. Previously, this was the northern remote territory of México. The area covered the land from California to Tejas, which was thousands of square miles. Before the Mexican-American War, México was geographically larger than the United States. After the war, the United States became larger than México. And on this land, the United States also acquired a population of Mexican people. The United States was more than willing to take the territory from México. However, it was not as willing to assimilate *Mexicanos,* whose language and culture differed greatly from that of the United States.

As a result of the Mexican-American War, Mexicans became citizens of the United States according to the Treaty of Guadalupe Hidalgo. Thus, *Mexican American* became the denotation for these new citizens under the colonizing country. The United States was the colonizer and the *Mexicanos* the colonized. Mexican culture and daily lifestyle revolved around agriculture of sorts. Small ranching and farming was the norm along with *vaquero* culture. Mexicans were hard-working *pobladores* living in the countryside or in small towns, *pueblos.* Many *pobladores* were also *los pobres,* the working poor. Most of these towns were originally established as part of the old mission system, such as Los Angeles and San Antonio. As previously stated, Mexicans now found themselves in a different society. Perhaps they assumed that life would go on as usual and that their Mexican culture would exist and survive much as it did before the war. Maybe they assumed, "We survived when this was Nueva España, we survived when this was México, and therefore, we will survive as part of the United States." Depending on their individual circumstance, some Mexicans were pleasantly surprised, others found it a shocking experience, and others were shocked to death. Their destiny remained to be seen.

Following the war, U.S. social, cultural, economic, and political structures moved into what became the Southwest. The arriving immigrants to Aztlán called themselves *Americans* in reference to the United States of America. It appeared that these newcomers had very little regard for Mexicans and *Mexicano* culture. This resulted in a harsh social and cultural clash between Americans and Mexicans. Obviously, the Americans were the ones who controlled the new power structure. As the Mexican system changed to American society, *Mexicanos* started feeling like second-class citizens, strangers in their own land, and people without a country. Prejudice, discrimination, and racism against *Mexicanos* became commonplace in the new Southwest.

A few Mexicans attempted to assimilate into the new American social order and power structure. Generally, these were the rich and well-to-do Mexicans, *los ricos.* Mexicans previously involved in economics, politics and governance attempted to integrate. A new American social and cultural system was imposed and overlaid on a land that was previously the northern territories of México. Throughout the American Southwest, a few Mexicans ran for and were elected to statewide office. They were soon voted out, in most cases. Mexican participation in the societal and political system was dependent on the waves of anti-Mexican fervor prevalent at the time. Entrepreneurial Mexicans benefited by aligning themselves economically and politically with rich Americans. This included marriages between well-to-do American men and Mexican women. In *North from México,* Carey McWilliams stated, "Becoming rich from the commerce which developed after the opening of the Santa Fe Trail, many looked with favor upon closer ties with the Anglo-Americans."[1] Assimilation into American society proved beneficial for *los ricos* and other Mexicans involved in trade and commerce.

During this period of time, some Mexicans had their land confiscated by the United States through government officials. Mexicans lost their land at the hands of American courts, judges, and lawyers. There are cases of Mexicans being driven off their land by gun-wielding Americans. They lost their land through force or trickery. Many a Spanish-speaking *Mexicano* had an impossible time attempting to protect his property land claim before American officials. Land originally belonging to Mexicans was sold for pennies on the dollar. The Mexican land was acquired by American companies such as these:

- Land companies, who rushed to the Southwest immediately after the war
- Agricultural and ranching companies
- Mining companies
- Railroad companies

According to McWilliams, individuals such as Richard King of the famous King Ranch in Texas amassed sprawling acres in the hundreds of thousands.[2] The Southwest became very profitable to American business and commercial enterprise. This was an economic boom for the United States and a ghastly nightmare for *los pobres pobladores.*

As a result and consequence of the Mexican-American War, *Mexicanos* found themselves living in a hostile environment. In the late 1800s, violence and brutality toward *Mexicanos* was so common as to almost pass unnoticed by American society. By gunslingers to police, they were killed to the old rallying cry of *Remember the Alamo* and *Remember Goliad.* Shooting of Mexicans by law enforcement was the norm, no questions asked. The attitude and practice of marshals and sheriffs amounted to *shoot first, ask questions later.* In court, it appeared as though Mexicans were guilty until proven innocent. Lynching was so common as to almost pass unnoticed during this time of *the good old western days.* Many Mexicans were forced to segregate themselves into their own communities for the sake of survival. In the safety and security of their own *barrios,* Mexican culture continued and even flourished. It could be argued that Mexicans in the United States existed as a separate society after the Mexican-American War. This was a sad chapter in the annals of American history.

Mexicanos living under the invasion and colonization by the United States reacted in various fashions. As previously discussed, *los ricos* attempted assimilation into American society. Many Mexicans, however, felt like second-class citizens, strangers in their own land, and people without a country. Living in a hostile environment led to revolt and revolution by *Mexicanos* against United States authority. Mexicans rebelling against the colonization, subjugation, and domination were declared bandits and outlaws by American society. Nonetheless, to many *Mexicanos,* the rebels who questioned and defied American authority became legendary folk heroes, like *Robin Hood.*

Some of the best known and infamous *social bandits* included:

Elfego Baca in Texas (born in New México)

Gregorio Cortez in Texas

Joaquín Murrieta in California

Juan "Cheno" Cortina in Texas

Sostenes L'Archeveque in New México

Tiburcio Vásquez in California

Sadly for some Mexicans, one day they were landowners and pillars of the community, and the next day declared outlaws by the United States. Americans turned vigilantes had no qualms lynching *Mexicanos* suspected of a crime. To begin with, Mexicans *were* suspect. This era of lawlessness and brutality had dire consequences for Mexicans and far-reaching ramifications for race and ethnic relations in the United States.

A case in point is the story of Tiburcio Vásquez. He came from a well-known and highly respected family. His grandfather helped found San Francisco and his father was the first mayor of San José, California. *Californios* were alarmed and rightly concerned about the invading hordes of gold-starved Yankees. The pivotal incident occurred when Tiburcio went to a dance with friends. Apparently, there was a fight involving Yankees. A lawman was called in. The lights went out, and suddenly the lawman was dead. Tiburcio, Anastacio García, and José Guerra were implicated. The latter were lynched and Tiburcio fled. Thus began the adventures and escapades of a wanted man. In *Drink Cultura,* José Antonio Burciaga has written:

> *According to Stanford University history professor Albert Camarillo, "Vásquez created fear in the Anglos because of his revolutionary potential. Tiburcio, on at least one occasion, had ambitions of effecting an uprising or revolution against the 'Yankee invaders of California.' He stated that 'given $60,000, I would be able to recruit enough arms and men to revolutionize Southern California.' Indeed, Tiburcio Vásquez was able to free himself of the Anglo colonization and become a 'quasi-bandit revolutionary.'" In fact, to the end, Vásquez had hoped that before hanging he would have a chance to make a speech on the scaffold, calling for a revolution.[3]*

Tiburcio Vásquez became a legendary folk hero in the eyes of many *Mexicanos.*

These folk heroes have emerged as part of the folklore of the Southwest. Many a *corrido* (folk ballad) has been sung telling these stories and passing on the oral history to future generations. These folk heroes are remembered by their respective communities throughout the

Southwest. Another case in point is the story of Gregorio Cortéz. His life is commemorated in *El Corrido de Gregorio Cortéz.* The *corrido* was turned into a motion picture in 1982 titled *The Ballad of Gregorio Cortéz,* starring Edward James Olmos. The movie by Chicano filmmaker Moctezuma Esparza was based on the book *With a Pistol in His Hand: A Border Ballad and Its Hero* by Américo Paredes.[4] Another folk hero is Joaquín Murrieta in California. According to the narrative, he was a landowner forced to flee at the hands of Anglo Americans. His family was attacked and he lost his land. One account says that his young wife was gang raped by the intruders. With a sense of revenge, he went after those who had destroyed his life and family. The state of California put a reward on his head, *dead or alive.* Stories abound regarding the deeds and exploits of the legendary Joaquín Murrieta. Every summer, there is a celebration with a march by horseback on the west side of the San Joaquin Valley. It has become a tradition to commemorate the life and times of Joaquín Murrieta. From the Chicano-Latino perspective, Joaquín Murrieta, Gregorio Cortéz, and the others mentioned are a significant part of Mexican American history. The Mexican folklore of the Southwest *is* part of American history and should be recognized by all.

Note to Students   Do you feel it is culturally important to celebrate these legendary folk heroes? Why or why not?

THE MEXICAN CONTRIBUTION IN BUILDING THE SOUTHWEST

Regardless of the fact that many Mexicans felt the cultural clash of living in a hostile society, they nonetheless integrated themselves into the economy due to their labor. Mexicans worked hard, whether or not it was acknowledged by the country. Mexicans labored in harsh conditions building the economic foundation of the Southwest. They did a massive amount of backbreaking work with bare hands, picks and shovels. It is likely that American society had little regard for *Mexicano* culture but was more than willing to exploit the people for the ready supply of cheap labor. It appears that in the Southwest, Mexicans did the majority of labor in the crucial areas, including agriculture and ranching, mining, and railroad building.

Mexican Americans provided the backbreaking labor that was necessary at the turn of the century in building the economic infrastructure of the Southwest of the United States. The emergence of American capitalism was made possible by the exploitation of labor, which resulted in great wealth for American society. From the Chicano-Latino perspective, Mexican labor was a major contribution to building the infrastructure of this country.

CONCLUSION

The 1800s proved to be a trying time for *Mexicanos* in Aztlán. The forces that impacted their life ranged from social and cultural change to conflict. México was born a new country economically and was politically bankrupt after three hundred years of colonization by Spain.

The economic disaster in México and the political turmoil in México City proved devastating for the country. Living in the far remote northern territories of México, the *Mexicanos* in the different locations developed a unique and distinct cultural identity of their own. These *Mexicanos* in Aztlán were survivors. Through thick or thin, war, feast, or famine, they managed to survive. Regardless of the challenge, they endured with the power and strength of *familia*. *Mexicanos* and Mexican culture seem to have emerged stronger than ever. The question now was, were they ready to face the turn of the century, the Industrial Revolution, and American capitalism?

CHAPTER DISCUSSION QUESTIONS

1. Discuss the life of *Mexicanos* before the Mexican-American War.

2. Discuss the life of *Mexicanos* after the Mexican-American War:

3. What social and cultural changes affected the life of *Mexicanos*?

4. What are examples of cultural conflict?

5. What does it mean to be colonized by another country?

6. What were the results and consequences of the war? For México? For the United States?

7. What were the far-reaching implications and ramifications of the war?

8. *We didn't cross the border; the border crossed us!* When Mexican Americans make this statement, what does it mean?

9. Why do Mexican Americans claim to be an indigenous population in Aztlán?

© Betacam-SP/Shutterstock.com

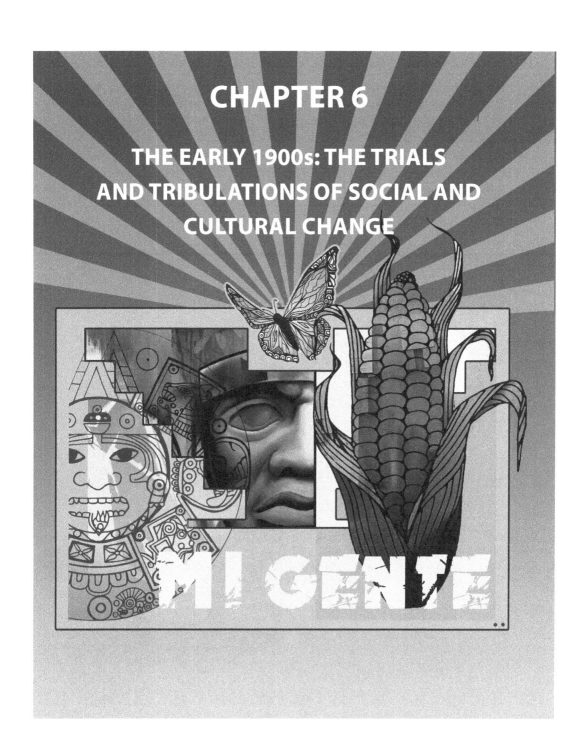

CHAPTER 6

THE EARLY 1900s: THE TRIALS AND TRIBULATIONS OF SOCIAL AND CULTURAL CHANGE

THE MEXICAN REVOLUTION OF 1910: ¡VIVA LA REVOLUCIÓN!

The story of Aztlán and La Raza takes a detour as we visit our brothers and sisters back in México. The revolution in México had far-reaching implications, not only for *Mexicanos* in that country, but for Mexicans in the United States. The revolution caused a civil unrest, leading to a bloody civil war that tore the country apart.

Why a revolution? President Porfirio Díaz oversaw a brutal thirty-plus-year dictatorship. The rich and wealthy Mexican elite loved Porfirio Díaz. The president was thrusting México into the modern age of the Industrial Revolution. Who would question the benefit of México's modernization? Great wealth was created during the years of President Díaz by

the exploitation of the workers. The poor working class was condemned to slave labor. The wealthy and powerful got rich on the backs of *los pobres peones*. The elite ruling class were the rich landowners. They owned the labor and they owned the land. A very small percentage of the population owned the great majority of the land. The rich got richer and the poor got poorer. Díaz opened México to foreign investors, especially U.S. companies that came in to exploit the labor. The American government and entrepreneurs supported Díaz and the ruling class. The United States subsequently intervened on behalf of American business interests.

Of all the famous revolutionaries, Emiliano Zapata and Francisco "Pancho" Villa are especially remembered. Zapata was probably the most influential leader, due to his ideology. This involved agrarian land reform, as declared in his famous *Plan de Ayala*. For Zapata, the mission of the revolution was land and liberty, *Tierra y Libertad*. Emiliano fought in the south against *los federales*. These federal troops were sent by the president to capture or kill Zapata. Pancho Villa fought *los federales* in the north. Villa gathered an army of the poor to fight against the government. Díaz hated Villa and seemed to consider him more bandit than revolutionary. The exploits of Pancho Villa turned into a mixture of fact and folklore as stories circulated regarding this vibrant antigovernment rebel. From the perspective of the revolutionaries, the wealthy *Mexicano* elite stole the land from *los peones*, the peons. Emiliano Zapata and Pancho Villa symbolized the spirit of the Mexican Revolution. This was a struggle of poor working-class people trying to liberate themselves from the oppression and tyranny of the government. Zapata and Villa were eventually assassinated.

After President Díaz was overthrown in the violent revolution, Francisco Madero was elected president. Madero was the *apostle of democracy*. Francisco wanted democracy for the country and the people. Madero was an educated man from the upper class. He even studied at the University of California–Berkeley for a time. Madero was very intelligent, but a political reformer more than a revolutionary. Yes, people wanted democracy, but first they were hungry for food and productive land. This required yet another overthrow of the government and the elite ruling class. Madero was eventually assassinated.

Women played an astounding role in the Mexican Revolution. They fought on the battlefield side by side with the men. These woman soldiers were *soldaderas*. Some became leaders and generals. It is traditional to remember these brave and courageous women as *Las Adelitas*.

The bloody civil war devastated the country, brother against brother. From ideological factions to the overthrow of presidents and military leaders, México was divided. Political upheaval and economic devastation befell the country.

A significant number of *Mexicano* families exited the country to get away from the chaos and confusion and fled to the United States. They crossed the border with whatever they could carry, satisfied to escape with their lives. These refugees had no choice but to leave their brothers and sisters behind.

There were many heroes and villains before, during, and after the Mexican Revolution on all and every side of the civil war. Among the famous and infamous people of this era included:

Joaquín Amaro

Mariano Azuela

Francisco S. Carbajal

Lázaro Cárdenas

Venustiano Carranza

Antonio Caso

Carlos Chávez

Ramón Corral

Adolfo de la Huerta

Genovevo de la O

Féliz Díaz

Pablo González

Roque González Garza

Jesús Guajardo

Eulalio Gutiérrez

Martín Luis Guzmán

Victoriano Huerta

Francisco Lagos Cházaro

Pedro Lascuráin

Francisco León de la Barra

José Limantour

José López Portillo y Rojas

Enrique Flores Magón

Ricardo Flores Magón

Alvaro Obregón

José Clemente Orozco

Pascual Orozco

José Pino Suárez

José Guadalupe Posada

Alfonso Reyes

Bernardo Reyes

Diego Rivera

Justo Sierra

David Alfaro Siqueiros

Don Luis Terrazas

Teresa Urrea

José Vasconcelos

Leaders, artists, intellectuals, presidents, despots, soldiers, and revolutionaries, one and all participated in a bloody revolution, and tens of thousands died. It was a great human tragedy for México. Every year *Mexicanos* commemorate *Día de la Revolución* on the 20th of November. The spirit, triumph, and catastrophe of the revolution haunts México to this day.

Note to Students   Do historical and cultural research by investigating the life and times of protagonists from the list above. Research the intriguing role of women revolutionaries.

BACK TO AZTLÁN AND *MEXICANOS* IN THE *GOOD OLD U.S.A.*

Life continued with many challenges for Mexicans in the United States during the early 1900s.

This statement in *North from Mexico* by Carey McWilliams is quite astounding and revealing:

> *Open Season on Mexicans. In an article in World's Work, George Marvin reported that "the killing of Mexicans . . . through the border in these last four years is almost incredible. . . . Some rangers have degenerated into common man-killers. There is no penalty for killing, for no jury along the border would ever convict a white man for shooting a Mexican. . . . Reading over the Secret Service records makes you feel almost as though there were an open game season on Mexicans along the border.[1]*

At the turn of the century, prejudice, discrimination, and racism was the sad and unfortunate reality for *Mexicanos* in American society.

The new century was especially known for the impact of the Industrial Revolution in American society. Among the many new changes of the Industrial Revolution were:

Electricity

Cars and the internal combustion engines

Locomotives for transportation and moving cargo

Factories, the assembly line, and mass production

Industrialization

Urbanization

Modernization

American capitalism

The many social and cultural changes revolutionized daily life in the United States. This included a population movement from the rural to the urban. In this shift, people left the farming countryside and moved to the cities. City life for many became the norm. The Industrial Revolution swept in a new era for American society and culture.

The United States saw a proliferation of ethnic enclaves in the city. This refers to ethnic communities with their own unique and distinct culture. Immigrants from all over the world arrived in the U.S. and created their own ethnic cultural neighborhoods—for example, Chinatown, French Quarter, Greek Town, Jewish Quarter, Little Italy, and Polish Town. The Czechs, Germans, Irish, Russians, Swedes, and everyone else from around the world were immigrating to América. Mexicans called their communities *El Barrio* or *La Colonia*. Sometimes they preferred a nickname such as *La Chancla* or Tortilla Flats. These were names for Mexican neighborhoods used to identify their distinct cultural communities. The ethnic communities served as a settlement process for immigrants adapting to a new country. Later, second and third generations assimilated and Americanized into the mainstream. Some, of course, assimilated more easily than others.

As discussed in the previous chapter, *Mexicanos* interwove themselves into the American economic fabric through their labor in a variety of working-class jobs. This pattern continued in the 1900s with Mexicans contributing their work in rural *and* urban América. *Mexicanos* still worked in agriculture, farming, and ranching. They continued to contribute their skills. For instance, they were among the best sheepherders, *pastores,* in the Southwest. Mexicans worked in the huge mining operations of the Southwest, including coal, copper, iron ore, and all others. Working on the railroad was a major occupation for many *Mexicanos*. Thousands of miles of railroad were built with picks and shovels and bare hands. Mexicans were instrumental in the construction of roads, highways, and bridges to accommodate vehicles with the internal combustion engine. In the city, *Mexicanos* worked in the construction and building industry of the new urban sprawl. The trades and industry required manual labor. Mexicans took much pride in their work, and more work. Life was hard, but they found strength in family and culture.

WORLD WAR I, 1914 TO 1918, AND THE AFTERMATH

This was known as the *Great War* and the *War to End All Wars*. World War I created a boom economy for the United States. Mexicans participated in the war effort in two ways. First, they joined the military to fight for the country. They became American soldiers. Second, Mexican labor continued to be a vital factor within the American economy of the Southwest. American capitalism and modernization required mass labor. This was doubly imperative with the war effort. Mexicans were employed in many fields and contributed their manual labor.

At this juncture, immigration from México was a major factor. This can be analyzed with the concept of *push-pull factors*. Mexicans were being *pushed* away from México due to the chaos and confusion of the revolution. At the same time, they were being *pulled* to the United States due to the need for workers during a boom economy. Another concept or model for analysis is the idea of *ebb and flow of migration*. This means the movement back and forth between the two countries was based on people's needs, such as jobs. Mexicans arrived in the United States and assimilated themselves into the open job market. Generally, these were the hardest and lowest-paying jobs. Discrimination in the workplace was a common experience for many *Mexicanos*.

After WWI, there was a downturn in the economy of the United States. The war was costly in terms of dollars and cents and human casualties. American soldiers coming home prompted displacement and unemployment. It appeared that in the slowing economy, some were searching for answers. Some were asking, "What are all these Mexicans doing here?" McWilliams wrote:

> *Readers' Guide lists fifty-one articles on "the Mexican Problem" from 1920 to 1930. . . . In other words, "the Mexican Problem" has been defined in terms of the social consequences of Mexican immigration. . . . With the passage of the 1924 Immigration Act, the immigrant social agencies and Americanization institutes simply had to discover a new "problem" and it was the Mexican's misfortune to appear on the scene. . . . As a consequence, he was promptly adopted as America's No. 1 immigrant problem.[2]*

As already illustrated, Mexicans were defined as a "problem" in the eyes of many. In an economic slowdown, *Mexicanos* were a convenient scapegoat. This was a real slap in the face for Mexicans. To begin with, *Mexicanos* had their cultural roots planted in Aztlán prior to the annexation by the United States. In addition, the life of Mexicans revolved around work, and therefore their labor contributed to the economic infrastructure.

The debate of Mexicans and Mexican immigration took center stage with politicians. A pervasive attitude emerged on the American scene. "Why are all these Mexicans here? Mexicans are taking everyone's jobs! Mexicans are ruining the economy! Send them back to Mexico!" This went hand in hand with the founding of the United States Border Patrol in 1924. The creation of the Border Patrol was at the juncture when the focus pointed at the Mexican border and the *Mexican problem*. One could make a strong argument that an undercurrent of racism was guiding the entire debate. Looking at American history, these were not *Happy Days* for race and ethnic relations in the United States.

THE STOCK MARKET CRASH OF 1929 AND THE GREAT DEPRESSION OF THE 1930s

Americans might relate the Great Depression to the famous classic novel, *The Grapes of Wrath* by John Steinbeck. The Depression era exacerbated the anti-Mexican and anti-immigrant fervor. The U.S. government responded to the negative American sentiment by engaging the Border Patrol. An interesting reference in examining the Depression is the movie *My Family, Mi Familia,* narrated by Edward James Olmos. The Hollywood movie was written and directed by Gregory Nava (New Line Cinema, 1995). There is a dramatic scene in which

María, played by actress Jennifer Lopez, is arrested by the Border Patrol. It matters not that she is pleading that she lives here and belongs here. The Border Patrol throws her in a railroad cattle car and deports her to México. As Edward James Olmos states in the movie:

> It was the time of the Great Depression. I guess some politicians got it into their heads that Mexicanos were responsible for the whole thing . . . so la migra made some big sweeps through the barrio and they rounded up everyone they could. It didn't matter if you were a citizen . . . if you looked Mexicano, you were picked up and shipped out. . . . All these things really happened. The year was 1933. The Southern Pacific Railroad made the U.S. government a deal. For $14.75 a head, they took the Mexicans all the way into central Mexico hoping they would never be able to get back.

By no means were *Mexicanos* the cause of the Great Depression! Once again, they were used as a convenient scapegoat. The movie underscores that thousands of Mexicans, including American citizens, were deported to México during these days. The relationship between the Border Patrol and the Mexican community is a controversial issue to this day. The Border Patrol, as an arm of the U.S. government, continues to promote a schism in American society.

THE 1940s

A significant percentage of *Mexicanos* have always lived in rural América. So, for instance, Mexicans did the majority of agricultural labor in the Southwest of the United States. Ranching and agriculture became interwoven with *Mexicano* culture. There were no fruits or vegetables not touched by a Mexican. They labored in all crops, including almonds, apples, apricots, asparagus, beans, berries, broccoli, cabbage, cherries, cotton, garlic, grapes, lettuce, lemons, melons, peaches, pears, peas, peppers, prunes, onions, oranges, spinach, strawberries, tomatoes, walnuts, and everything else! They did a lot of work in order to make a living and at the same time help feed the United States. The strong Mexican work ethic served the country well. Generally, *Mexicano* culture in rural América was homogeneous—that is, mostly similar cultural experiences.

However, a great number of *Mexicanos* now lived, worked, and played in the city urban environment. This posed some interesting challenges and opportunities in regard to life and culture. Would Mexicans in the city maintain their culture as in past generations? Would they continue to practice the traditional culture? The city definitely caused some changes in the lives of *Mexicanos* and their families.

Culture and family go through many changes with city life. Social and cultural change are always part of the dynamics. The parents and older generation may resist change and try to hold on to the traditional culture. The children and younger generation may want to adapt to what they see as a new, modern way of life. This causes generational differences and cultural conflict between the young and old. How did Mexicans reconcile the differences?

This was an era when Mexicans continued to live and participate in American society within the stress, strains, and friction of the time. Mexicans were hard at work doing the many manual jobs in a growing and expanding, modernizing capitalistic economy. The city provided people with the opportunity to change and modify life and culture. It appeared that some *Mexicanos* started to Americanize due to their experiences in this country. The Americanization process entailed adopting the lifestyle of the time, such as dress, music, and pop culture. Americanization translated to assimilation into the culture of the United States. Mexicans could attempt to assimilate, but was the country in the 1940s ready to integrate *Mexicanos* into the mainstream of American culture?

World War II

The United States entered the war in 1941 and was a major player until the end in 1945. Many Mexicans joined the military in large numbers to fight for their country. Mexicans, just like other Latinos, fought in every military theater of the war. They returned to the States as war heroes. Some came back walking, some in wheelchairs, and some in coffins. Overall, Latinos earned more than their share of Congressional Medals of Honor for valor in WWII. Many of these brave military men and women have only been recently recognized on the American scene. There are still many more unsung heroes. It goes without saying that among these families, the bravery of their sons and daughters is a source of much honor and pride.

Note to Students   For intense accounts of Mexican American involvement in the war effort, see books such as Raul Morin's *Among the Valiant* (Alhambra: Borden Publishing Company, 1966). Do research on Mexican and Latino veterans.

Who was Pvt. Felix Z. Longoria (1920–1945)? What was the Felix Longoria Affair?

Prejudice, Discrimination and Racism during the 1940s

Regardless of the fact that Mexicans fought and died in the war, they still faced prejudice and discrimination at home in the United States. To fight and die for your country was the ultimate expression of patriotism. It was a societal disgrace and embarrassment that signs in front of businesses read:

No Dogs or Mexicans Allowed

No Colored or Mexicans

Whites Only

Or, in front of a theater or dance ballroom, the sign might have read:

Wednesday: Mexican Night

Occasionally, a government office might have had two reception counters to serve the public, one with a sign *Whites* and the other *Colored*. This was very confusing for Mexicans, since they did not identify with either. Most times there was no need for a sign because *Mexicanos* quickly learned where they were and were not welcomed. This was a sad and unfortunate state of affairs for American society.

During the 1940s, segregation in the schools was a common occurrence in the southwestern United States. Sometimes it was official and sometimes it was not legal or official but the common practice of the schools. At times, Mexicans fought against segregation. One of the most famous cases was the *Westminster* case in Orange County, California. On behalf of parents, Gonzalo Méndez filed a lawsuit due to the fact that his children were forced to attend a separate and inferior *Mexican school*. After a difficult legal fight, the case was confirmed in favor of the Mexican children. In 1947, the judgment of the court deemed that segregation of Mexican students violated the equal protection clause of the Fourteenth Amendment. It was a great, successful battle, but the war against prejudice, discrimination, and racism in other venues continued.

An interesting reference to the situation of Mexicans in the 1940s is the example of the play *Zoot Suit*. This play, made into a film (Universal Pictures, 1982), was directed and produced by the famous playwright Luis Valdez, founder of El Teatro Campesino. It starred Edward James Olmos as *El Pachuco*. According to the story, *pachucos* were young Mexican Americans who created a cultural movement and lifestyle within the Mexican community. From the perception of these youths, they were navigating between two cultural worlds. They did not feel *Mexicano* like their *old-fashioned* parents, yet did not seem to fit into the mainstream American popular culture. Therefore, they fashioned their own cultural style for a new generation of Mexican Americans. They even developed their own dialect (*caló*) or language, known as *pachuquismo*. The *pachucos* wore sharp zoot suits and the *pachucas* wore matching attire. As *El Pachuco* stated in the movie, "The idea of the original chuco is to look like a diamond, to look sharp, hip, bonaroo, finding a style of urban survival in the rural skirts and outskirts of the brown metropolis of Los Angeles." The *pachuco* movement made a definite impact on the Mexican community, and American society was also affected by the racial state of affairs in the 1940s.

The movie *Zoot Suit* revolves around the infamous Sleepy Lagoon murder case in Los Angeles. This drama starts with the incident of the taxicab brigade. The newspapers and radio were running stories portraying *pachucos* as gangsters and criminals. These negative depictions alarmed the American public and fanned anti-Mexican and anti-immigrant sentiment. Soldiers from the local military bases decided to teach the zoot suiters a lesson. They rented a number of taxicabs and invaded the eastside Mexican barrio. Essentially, they were soldiers turned vigilantes. Touring the *barrio*, they stopped at the sight of zoot suiters. Young Mexican Americans dressed in *pachuco* fashion were accosted by the soldiers. The youth were left beaten and stripped of their clothes, only to be later arrested by the police. The newspapers called this episode the *Zoot Suit Riots*, but who was causing the commotion? The situation continued for several days until it was finally stopped due to the outcry by the Mexican American community and others. These *others* included the much-quoted author,

Carey McWilliams, then chairman of the Sleepy Lagoon Defense Committee. In the Sleepy Lagoon murder case, Henry Leyvas and his friends were accused of murdering José Díaz. They were railroaded in court and sentenced to life in San Quentin Prison. The verdict was eventually overturned by the court of appeals and they were released in 1945. Needless to say, the taxicab brigade and Sleepy Lagoon murder case left a bitter taste in the mouth of the Mexican community in Los Angeles. It appeared that after all these years, *Mexicanos* were still living in a hostile environment!

The prejudice toward *Mexicanos* in the 1940s was very disappointing and ironic. From one perspective, Mexicans were major contributors to the war effort and the economy. They lived in working-class families. How did traditional parents raise their children? Remember that at this time, children grew up in old-fashioned, traditional *familias* with traditional values. Families contributed to society, as was the norm. Adults worked and children went to school, which was the function of the family as a social institution. From another perspective, institutionalized racism continued to promote prejudice and discrimination. For instance, many perceived the schools and the educational system as not sensitive or receptive to *Mexicanos*. Who would argue that being physically and verbally punished for speaking Spanish was a friendly environment for children? Many students dropped out, were pushed out, and went directly to work. Regardless of their hard work, the high frequency of poverty added insult to injury. With life in the *barrio*, many Mexicans felt like marginal people and second-class citizens in American society. Thank goodness for *Mexicano* families and culture. They learned to cope and make the best of life.

THE 1950s: THE AMERICAN POP CULTURE ERA OF *HAPPY DAYS*!

Like previous eras, the 1950s continued to promote social and cultural change in the Mexican culture and community. Large traditional families were still the norm. Mexicans attempted to remain traditional, especially those living in rural areas. American society and culture affected and influenced *Mexicanos* in many ways. Some Mexicans attempted to assimilate into the mainstream of American society. Urbanization and the urban lifestyle made Americanization an option. The *barrio* became a unique and distinct cultural mixture and blending of Mexican and American cultures. During the 1950s, Mexicans with their strong work ethic continued to make a major contribution as part of the labor force in the Southwest of the United States.

The 1950s was also the era of the Korean War, which lasted between 1950 and 1953. Similarly to WWII, Mexicans joined in large numbers. At home, the economy was growing and Mexicans were doing their part. The wartime was a boom economy due to the military effort. As in previous wars, Mexicans did more than their fair share of fighting and dying for their country. Mexican GIs were fighting overseas and the other Mexicans were working hard at home.

<u>*Note to Students*</u> For an eye-opening account of discrimination go online to the PBS American Experience production of the movie *A Class Apart (2009)*. In a little-known case, Hernanandez v. Texas, Mexican American lawyers challenged Jim Crow-style discrimination in Texas. In 1954, the U.S. Supreme Court ruled that Mexican Americans were indeed a group. Therefore, Mexican Americans were entitled to equal protection under the 14 Amendment as *a class apart*.

OPERATION WETBACK: 1954 TO 1955

History seemed to repeat itself. Again, after the Korean War there was an economic downturn. And again, an ugly anti-Mexican and anti-immigrant outcry from some corners of the American public appeared on the scene. "What are all these Mexicans doing here? Mexicans are taking everyone's jobs! Mexicans are ruining the economy! Send them back to Mexico!" In response to the outcry, the U.S. government engaged the Border Patrol. This time, it was called *Operation Wetback.* The Border Patrol invaded and raided the Mexican community. To the Border Patrol, anyone looking Mexican was a suspect. Thousands of Mexicans were deported to México. These raids and repatriations were a slap in the face for the Mexican community. Many Mexican immigrants had established work and family in the United States. They were hard-working, law-abiding people. Remember that these were still the days of large, traditional Mexican families. One could argue that the U.S. Border Patrol became instrumental in divide and conquer. In other words, the controversy caused a split within the Mexican and Mexican American community. Some established Mexican Americans started thinking, "Maybe they're right! Maybe these Mexicans from Mexico are taking my job!" Operation Wetback planted a seed of distrust and suspicion within the community. It promoted an attitude of arrogance by some Mexican Americans that somehow they were *better* than the Mexicans from México. Politicians in the United States continued to promote the policy of blaming Mexican immigrants and using them as a scapegoat. This was another sad chapter in the annals of American history.

CONCLUSION

In the final analysis, Mexicans during the early 1900s did their best to navigate through the waters of society whether it was the good, the bad, or the ugly. It turned out to be decades of trials and tribulations and much social and cultural change for Mexicans in American society. Employment was tied to socioeconomic status and quality of life. Jobs ranged from working in farms, to city labor, factories, and the military. A case in point is in regard to *Mexicanos* and the military service. As American GIs, they experienced life outside the Mexican community. Returning home, they had a different perspective of themselves and their expectations of life.

Their veteran benefits had the potential to change their future, and it did for many. Mexicans did in fact have a wide range of societal experiences. Economically, some did better than others. A few but not many attended college. Some *Mexicanos* were able to climb the socioeconomic ladder by training in the trades and industry. This first half of the century was a time of much social and cultural change for Mexicans in the United States. Within the community, life was rich with family and culture. Cultural arts, music, and dance embellished the life of *Mexicanos* within their *familias. La cultura cura* meant that their Mexican culture kept them strong, healthy, and happy regardless of American society.

Note to Students   Investigate the cultural arts with origins in the early 1900's. They may include cultural artistic expressions such as the art of cooking Mexican food, the mariachi, conjunto, Tejano music, folklore, folklorico music and dance, the low rider movement, Mexican Americans in rock 'n' roll, Mexican religious art, and many more.

Interesting social phenomena occurred during the early 1900s. Mexicans from México immigrated directly to cities on the East Coast and in the Midwest of the United States. Examples included job opportunities in the Chicago area. They went to work in factories, manufacturing, steel mills, and on the railroad. At the same time, there were some Mexicans who left their homeland of Aztlán and went to work across the country. This included, for instance, Texas migrant farm workers. Where there was work to be done, there were Mexicans. The push-pull factors and the ebb and flow of migration had a definite impact on Mexican communities throughout the United States.

The turn of the century was a great learning experience that changed life forever. Mexicans would never be the same again. These decades posed challenges and opportunities. The challenges set the stage for the birth of an upcoming struggle called the *Chicano Movement*. The United States had yet to deal with the real issues of race and ethnic relations. A social and cultural revolution was about to confront American society. People across the country were thinking *civil rights* and *human rights*. Mexican Americans identifying as *Chicanos* and *Chicanas* were about to change world history.

CHAPTER DISCUSSION QUESTIONS

1. In what ways did the Mexican Revolution of 1910 affect and influence México and Mexicans in the United States?
2. Discuss and explain the life of Mexicans at the turn of the century and up to the 1950s.
3. Discuss the participation and involvement of Mexicans in America's wars. In what ways did this experience affect the Mexican community?
4. What do you think about the *pachuco* style created by Mexican youth in the 1940s?

5. Discuss the historical and contemporary relationship between the Mexican American community and the Border Patrol. Why do you think immigration is such a burning topic today?

Ocelotl

Ocelot or Jaguar

CHAPTER 7

THE CHICANO MOVEMENT: THE 1960s AND 1970s

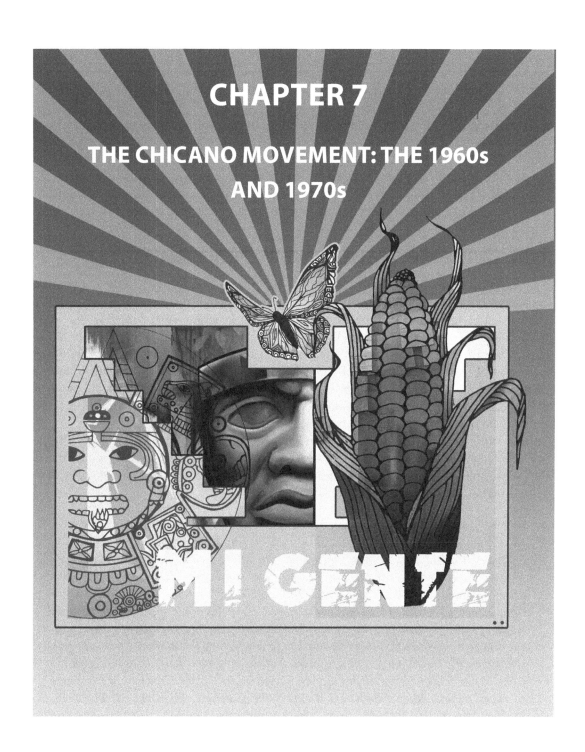

The 1960s and 1970s were a very memorable time for Mexican American history, heritage, and culture. Critical dynamics of change were occurring locally and nationally. These decades were a time of conflict and transformation for the United States. The dynamics ranged from assassinations to labor strikes, the Vietnam War, hippie culture, and the American civil rights movement. Some individuals were involved in political movements, while others created cultural revolutions, such as Carlos Santana and Little Joe and La Familia. Modern Chicano-Latino and traditional Mexican music and dance were creating an explosive cultural renaissance. Most people were affected by the dynamic social and cultural changes. Social movements prompted change, and certain elements of society resisted by adhering to the status quo. It was a time of challenge and opportunity for American society and culture.

1964: LAST YEAR OF THE BRACERO PROGRAM

An eyewitness of the 1960s was interviewed and questioned regarding what he remembered most about this decade. Of the many events of those years, his memory of the Bracero Program was a pivotal personal experience. The Bracero Program started in 1942 due to the critical need for workers during WWII. The so-called Bracero Program imported thousands of men from México to do work in the United States. From the perspective of unionized workers, this was an exploitation of labor. Most braceros worked in agriculture, laboring long hours from sunup to sundown. Working and living conditions were harsh, based on today's standards. There are many personal stories from survivors and their families. Braceros endured many sacrifices in order to help their families back in México.

The story of braceros was an important chapter in the life of many *Mexicanos*. This is a brief interview with a Chicano senior citizen. He worked in the fields as a farm worker during the last year of the Bracero Program. Here is his account of braceros picking tomatoes in the fields of Aztlán. This is an important story to tell:

In 1964, I was a 16-year-old kid doing farm labor. We used to call it working in the field. I had been a farm worker since the fifth grade during summer vacation from school. Summer vacation! That sounds funny now. Returning to school the teacher would ask us to write a composition on our summer vacation. Some of my classmates were writing about vacations at the beach, the city, Disneyland, camping, flying somewhere. For my composition, I WOULD LIE. I was embarrassed to say that I had spent the hot summer working out in the field like some peon. That summer, I witnessed braceros working in the field right next to us. I think I spent more time watching them, when I was supposed to be working. I was amazed and impressed at what I saw. I had already studied the Civil War in school even though I didn't understand it. The braceros looked like slaves to me, even though they did not have chains. Some of them were working without shirts, some without shoes, and some without hats. I remember the chill in the morning and the hot sun in the afternoon. When their lunch truck arrived, they ate in a few minutes and got back to work. They worked like machines or robots. For every box of tomatoes I picked, it seemed like they picked a dozen. When I arrived in the morning, they were already working. When I left in the afternoon, they were still working. They lived in old barns out in the country and slept in double bunk beds. I was very curious. I spent as much time as possible talking to them. They recounted some amazing stories about their life and family. As a young person, I was very touched by the sacrifice they were making in order to survive and better the life of their family back in México. I hope that some-day the governments of the United States and México hold an international ceremony to thank braceros for their service and contribution.

The Bracero Program is still controversial to this day. From the perspective of the survivors and their families, there is an issue of due compensation. The braceros had money deducted from their paycheck. This money was withheld and deposited in a special account. Braceros were to be paid in the future back in México. Some braceros have been partially compensated and others have not. For those now deceased, their surviving families are awaiting due compensation. There has been a movement afoot to pressure the United States and Mexican governments to do the right thing.

Note to Students Reading and Research. *Plane Wreck at Los Gatos* is the title of an old folk song. However this is the story of a real incident. On January 28, 1948 a plane wrecked at Los Gatos Canyon in Fresno County, California killed 32 people on board. Victims were the crew and 28 passengers being deported. It is thought some or most of the deportees were *braceros*. The 28 deportees were buried in a mass grave in Fresno at Holy Cross Cemetery. The headstone at the mass grave simply reads: *28 Mexican citizens who died in an airplane accident near Coalinga, California on Jan. 28, 1948 rip.* Can you imagine the grief of their family not knowing what happened to their loved ones in the United States?

THE CHICANO MOVEMENT OF THE 1960s AND 1970s

The 1960s and 1970s are often remembered for the famous and memorable *Chicano Movement*. This was a social movement that changed the very nature of the Mexican American community forever. The Chicano Movement was a movement to promote change in American society. The movement, *El Movimiento*, adopted the labels *Chicano* and *Chicana*. The parents of most Chicanos and Chicanas did not like these labels, which some thought meant lower-class Mexicans. The Chicano Movement gave these labels new social, cultural, and political definitions. Chicanos and Chicanas were Mexican Americans who saw themselves from a new dynamic perspective. Their imperative was to do a critical analysis of the history, heritage, and culture of Mexicans in the United States. Examining the history of social injustice and inequality was a consciousness-raising experience for Mexican Americans. In a sense, this was a radical awakening to the realities of the past. Chicanos and Chicanas decided that they would no longer accept and acquiesce to prejudice, discrimination, and racism. They experienced a radicalization process, meaning that they were willing to march, demonstrate, and protest in order to confront and change the system. For Mexican Americans to use the terms *Chicano* and *Chicana* was a matter of personal identity. Chicanos and Chicanas developed an ideology and philosophy of liberation from oppression, exploitation, social injustice, and inequality. This philosophy was *Chicanismo* and the struggle was *La Causa*, the cause.

The Chicano Movement was a social movement. This social movement was a collective group of people in an ongoing and continuous effort to promote social, cultural, and political change in society. The emphasis of the Chicano Movement was to advance the change necessary to make the social system sensitive and receptive to the needs of the Mexican American community. Chicanos and Chicanas represented a concerted effort to solve collectively problems they had in common. The notion of the day was *Chicano solutions to Chicano problems*.

The Chicano Movement did not arise out of a void in society. The movement was a direct reaction to social problems and conditions. There were a multiplicity of causes that created the need for a movement. The social conditions that gave rise to the Chicano Movement were economic and political oppression, interwoven with prejudice, discrimination, and racism. A significant number of Mexican Americans experienced a political radicalization process. The heightened social and cultural consciousness provided the spark for the social movement. The strength of the movement was culture, race, and ethnicity as an organizational concept. In other words, they could identify with *La Raza*, and that was the common denominator. The concepts of *Chicano*, *Chicana*, and *Chicano Movement* were conceptualized and popularized as the symbol of a new dynamic unity.

The Chicano Movement was one dimension of the American civil rights movement. People form social movements when they become dissatisfied and lose confidence in the system's ability to solve their problems. If people feel that the system can change, they then move into collective action. Thus was the situation for Chicanos and Chicanas. The purpose of the Chicano Movement was to make American society sensitive and receptive to the needs of a population previously ignored, neglected, and excluded. Ironically enough, Mexicans had a history of significant contributions to American society. Chicanos and Chicanas were involved in a struggle to fight for civil rights.

During the many years of American history, some Mexicans felt like strangers in their own land and second-class citizens. Many experienced a sense of powerlessness, marginality, alienation, and social isolation. This was especially true in relation to *barrio* life. People felt segregated from American society and culture. The Chicano quoted above regarding the Bracero Program was asked to give his personal definition of *second-class citizen*.

This anonymous writer wrote:

Is my existence outside the mainstream of American culture?
Why do I feel marginal? I'm on the outside looking in.
Why do I feel alienated? I'm alien, separate, apart, and away.

Why do I feel as an underclass? I'm trampled underneath someone's feet.
Why do I feel invisible? I'm not seen, my humanity is not visible to society.

Before there was Chicano-Latino Studies in college, an English professor assigned me to read the book Invisible Man *by Ralph Ellison.*[1] *Even though he was writing about African Americans, it felt like he was describing my existence growing up in a Mexican barrio. I was completely astounded by the imagery he presented. It was as though he was talking about my neighborhood. It was a complete eye opener and revelation to realize why I was invisible in the eyes of society. Why did I get involved in the Chicano Movement? Back in the day, we felt that American society was a hypocrite. As little kids we went to school and were forced to say the words "with liberty and justice for all." Yet we looked around the community and what did we see? Poverty, prejudice, discrimination, racism. The schools called us dropouts but in truth they pushed us out. We were condemned to the lowest rung of the social economic ladder. With the Chicano Movement, we confronted the system and promoted equal educational opportunity because we believed that education was the key to social mobility. Surprisingly enough, the issues of the Chicano Movement were not all that radical or revolutionary. In reality, Chicanos and Chicanas merely detested the oppression of prejudice, discrimination, racism, social inequality, and injustice. I believe history proved us right. In turn, the Chicano Movement struggled for the realization of economic and political democracy with full participation in American society and culture.*

This is the personal testimony of one person and his perception of life in American society. Of course, not all Mexican Americans think alike. They all have their individual perceptions of society. Social economic status and position, for instance, may be very influential in one's perspective of society. Thus, some Mexican Americans identified with the Chicano Movement and others did not. The Movement was famous to some and infamous to others.

Note to Students Field research. Interview working-class members of your community. Ask the questions: What is your definition of a second-class citizen? What does it mean to be outside the mainstream of American society and culture? Compare and contrast the responses you receive.

AMERICAN CIVIL RIGHTS MOVEMENT

In U.S. history, the era of the American civil rights movement was a pivotal time. The country experienced a social and cultural revolution. American society saw the anti–Vietnam War movement, the student movement, the Black Power movement, the women's movement, the hippie movement, and other collective groups. People felt that American society *was* the problem and they were willing to confront the system. The power structure at that time was resisting change and adhering to the status quo. People of all colors across the country were marching, demonstrating, protesting, and picketing. Confrontation and debate regarding civil rights was a major issue during these days.

Viva Kennedy!

Two individuals that had a significant impact on the political socialization of Chicanos and Chicanas were John F. Kennedy and Robert "Bobby" Kennedy. Many Mexican Americans were involved in the *Viva Kennedy* campaigns of the time. John F. Kennedy was the thirty-fifth president of the United States from 1961 to 1963. Mexican Americans fell in love with JFK as the first Catholic president and because of his image as a family man. He was perceived as the first president to acknowledge and communicate with Mexican Americans. His assassination came as a great shock and disappointment to *La Raza*. Here was a president they could relate to, and now he was gone. Afterward many Mexican Americans worked on the *Viva Kennedy* presidential campaign for his younger brother, Bobby. In fact, he was closer to the Mexican American community than JFK. People have fond memories of Bobby meeting with César Chávez and supporters of the United Farm Workers. They joined in the fight for social justice for farm worker families. The assassination of Robert Kennedy was another nightmare and devastation. Bobby was a presidential candidate who made a real and sincere effort to communicate and interact with the Chicano-Latino community. With John and Robert Kennedy, Mexican Americans became involved with national politics, and this learning experience was the real meaning of political socialization.

The Black Power Movement

Chicanos and Chicanas observed the unfolding and development of the Black Power movement. Across América everyone watched on television as African Americans marched for civil rights. Americans also saw African Americans attacked for daring to protest and demonstrate. African Americans learned to utilize race as an organizational concept in order to build their movement. They were organizing the community with rallying cries of *Black Power*, *Black is Beautiful*, and *Black Pride*. By the same token, Chicanos and Chicanas organized and mobilized with the concepts of *Chicano Power*, *Brown Power*, *Brown is Beautiful*, and *Brown Pride*. Similar to the Black Power movement, the Chicano Movement evolved and developed into a dynamic movement by utilizing culture, race, and ethnicity as an organizational concept. Community organizing was the approach for getting people involved in fighting for their civil rights.

CHICANO AND CHICANA LEADERS AND ORGANIZATIONS

During the 1960s and 1970s, there was a proliferation of organizations in the Mexican American community. They were dealing with a wide variety of community issues and social problems. Most of the active organizations identified with the Chicano Movement and the philosophy of *Chicanismo*. The Chicano Movement was, by definition, a very political movement. To be political meant to *rock the boat* and confront society to force change. The people involved in this were sometimes labeled *activists, militants*, *radicals*, or *revolutionaries*. However, a few of the organizations were more conservative. This meant that they hesitated to confront the system outright. Occasionally, they refused or maybe were embarrassed to join the marches, protests, demonstrations, and picketing. On the personal level, individuals may have been concerned about jeopardizing their job, status, and position acquired in society. They would generally comment, "It is better to work inside the system rather than confronting it from the outside."

Here is a partial list of student and community organizations involved in social issues. Some organizations of the era were founded before the main thrust of the Chicano Movement.

AMAE, Association of Mexican American Educators

American GI Forum

Brown Berets

CFMN, Comisión Femenil Mexicana Nacional

LULAC, League of United Latin American Citizens

MALDEF, Mexican American Legal Defense and Education Fund

MAPA, Mexican American Political Association

MASC, Mexican American Student Confederation

MAYO, Mexican American Youth Organization

MEChA, Movimiento Estudiantil Chicano de Aztlán

NCLR, National Council of La Raza

PASSO, Political Association of Spanish-Speaking Organizations

UMAS, United Mexican American Students

Each organization had its own agenda and focus. Some were more conservative and others more change oriented. The latter aligned themselves with the concept of *Chicanismo* as an ideology of liberation and self-determination. Not all the organizations agreed as to the tactics and strategies for changing the system.

Here is a partial list of individuals identified with the Chicano Movement. There was a proliferation of leaders in all communities. People saw the need to solve problems, and they answered the call by getting involved at the community level.

César Chávez, founder, United Farm Workers of America

Dolores Huerta, founder, United Farm Workers of America

　　　She coined the UFW rally cry: *Sí Se Puede!*[2]

Bert Corona, leader in MAPA and La Raza Unida Party

Mexican Independence Day Parade.

Rubén Salazar, reporter killed at the Chicano Moratorium, August 29, 1970, Los Angeles, California

Sal Castro, teacher involved in the 1968 Los Angeles high school walkouts (For an excellent reference see the HBO movie, *Walkout* [Executive producer, Moctezuma Esparza, 2008]).

José Angel Gutierrez, La Raza Unida Party, Crystal City, Texas

Reies López Tijerina, Allianza Federal de Pueblos Libres, New México

Rodolfo "Corky" Gonzalez, Crusade for Justice, Denver, Colorado; author of the Chicano epic poem *Yo Soy Joaquín*

The Chicano Movement created many leaders and community organizations. Chicanos and Chicanas organized and mobilized when they saw a need to promote civil rights and human rights. They also published a significant number of newsletters, newspapers, periodicals, and books related to *El Movimiento* and *La Causa*.

Note to Students   Readers are encouraged to do library and online research on the many leaders and organizations related to the Chicano Movement.

Note to Students   Reading and Research. *El Plan De Santa Barbara, A Chicano Plan For Higher Education* was published in 1969. The plan was adopted at a symposium at UC Santa Barbara as the founding document creating Chicano Studies. The Chicano student movement and MEChA were the dynamic force behind the creation of Chicano Studies.

Do research on: *El Plan Espiritual de Aztlán*. This was a manifesto adopted at the First National Chicano Liberation Youth Conference in Denver, Colorado, March 1969, hosted by Rodolfo *Corky* Gonzalez. The young Chicano Poet, Alurista was a moving speaker at this convention.

CÉSAR CHÁVEZ

The leader who was probably the most symbolic icon of the Chicano struggle was César Chávez (1927–1993). He was the founder of the United Farm Workers of America. Chávez was a very intelligent man, yet humble in a spiritual way. He was also a deeply religious person. He dedicated his entire life to improving the working conditions of farm working families. Farm workers do the labor to feed the country and therefore merit equal protection under the law. This includes a fair and reasonable salary; fair and reasonable working conditions; the right to collective bargaining; protection from harmful pesticides; unemployment insurance; and fringe benefits and a retirement plan. His greatness made him a powerful symbol of the fight for civil and human rights for farm workers. César died on April 23, 1993. His birthday on March 31 is a state holiday in California and several states, known as César Chávez Day.

Note to Students   Please Google the following to learn about the ideas of César Chávez: *Prayer of the Farm Workers' Struggle*.

CHICANO AND CHICANA CULTURAL RENAISSANCE

The Chicano Movement created an explosive cultural renaissance. Chicanos and Chicanas exploded into a cultural rebirth and enlightenment. Art and artistic expression reached a distinct and unique cultural dimension. Artistic talent, creativity, and imagination were unleashed. Art, music, dance, literature, poetry, *teatro*, film, and other art forms reflected the newly rediscovered *Brown Pride.* Throughout Aztlán a proliferation of artists expressed their cultural visions and reality through art. The multitude of artists of these days includes ASCO, mural-performance artists; Judith F. Baca, The Great Wall of Los Angeles; Luis Valdez, El Teatro Campesino; Royal Chicano Air Force, painters and muralists; and many, many more. For instance, the music of the time invigorated the energy of the people. Many Chicanos and Chicanas marched and protested to the beat of *Las Nubes*, the Clouds. This song by Little Joe and La Familia expressed the dreams and aspirations of the people. Symbolically, *Las Nubes* became the anthem of the Chicano Movement, along with the song classic *Yo Soy Chicano*. Thus, artists created art with a passion that reflected their history, heritage, and culture. Chicano and Chicana creativity resulted in a cultural arts revolution influential to this day.

CONCLUSION

El Movimiento was very idealistic and visionary. People fought for *La Causa*. The ultimate goal of the Chicano Movement was to end prejudice, discrimination, and racism. They fought for liberation from oppression and exploitation. Chicanos and Chicanas struggled to bring about social justice, equity, and equal opportunity. They believed the words *with liberty and justice for all* should be reality and not rhetoric. Chicanos and Chicanas strove to end poverty by promoting educational opportunity for all. They fought for self-determination and empowerment. So in the final analysis, what were the results and consequences of the

Chicano Movement? Were the dreams and aspirations of the Chicano Movement realized? *This is the continuing story of Aztlán and La Raza.*

CHAPTER DISCUSSION QUESTIONS

1. What was the Bracero Program? Answer: What, When, Where, Why, How?
2. Why did some Mexican Americans start calling themselves Chicanos and Chicanas?
3. What was the Chicano Movement all about?
4. What is the purpose of being involved in a social movement and in a political movement?

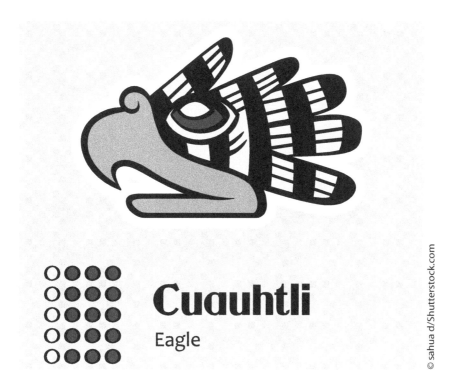

Cuauhtli

Eagle

© sahua d/Shutterstock.com

CHAPTER 8

MEXICAN AMERICANS: EXISTENCE, ASPIRATIONS AND EDUCATION IN THE TWENTY-FIRST CENTURY
BY FRANK PADILLA

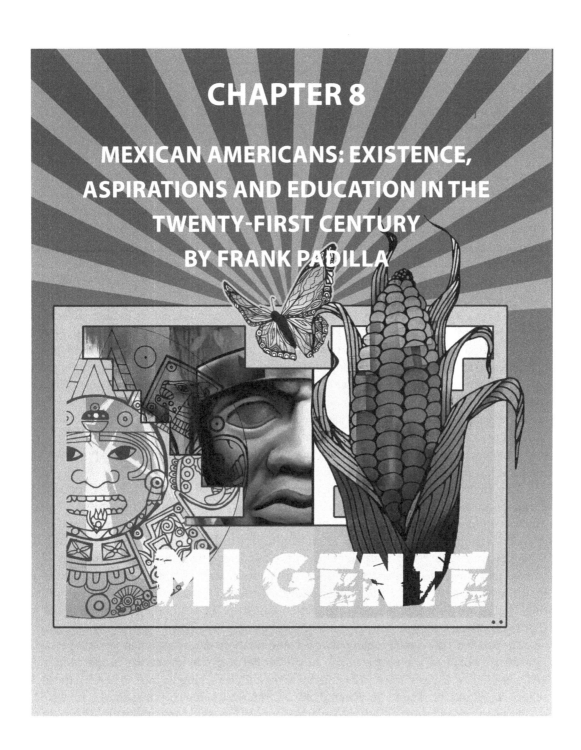

Latinos of the Twenty First Century have become the majority minority in the state of California and other states in the southwest. This is a reflection of a historical presence of Mexican Americans in former territories of Mexico before the Mexican American War in 1846-1848. Although the population has increased and the current century has brought many benefits, many inequities still exist.

The term *Latino/a* will be used when referring to the statistics so as to separate this minority group from the others. According to the most recent 2010 Census (www.census.gov), Latinos make up 17.1% percent or 54.5 million of the total population living in the United States. In some states they are the majority minority because of a longstanding history of living in these states and not merely a recent influx of migration into these areas. What is different in this century is the location of where Latino families live or call home. They are no longer limited to California and the southwestern states as they had previously. They now populate such states as Delaware, Nebraska, Kansas, and Wyoming, which generally tended to have a low percentage of Latinos (www.ed.gov.olea). Job opportunities in those states are attracting a new population that is willing to work the low pay or status jobs.

The Mexican American War of 1846-1848 allowed the United States to take almost half of Mexico's territories in the north. The future states of California, Colorado, New Mexico, Nevada, Arizona, Utah, and Texas were all once land belonging to Mexico. Each of the territories contained inhabitants from Mexico who after the war became strangers in their own land. Although they might have been considered "new Americans" because of where they lived, now because of indifference, language, or racism, they were not easily assimilated into mainstream society. Language became one of the major obstacles to assimilation. This issue would play throughout the history of Mexicans, Mexican Americans and any other immigrants who spoke Spanish. One of the solutions offered to ameliorate this problem was the Treaty of Guadalupe Hidalgo.

After the war, the inclusion of Mexicans as citizens of the new territories of the United States was given serious consideration. The Treaty of Guadalupe Hidalgo was ratified by the Mexican congress in 1848. One of the stipulations in the treaty was that the conquered Mexican citizens were to be granted full citizenship rights in the United States. When the U.S. Senate discussed the treaty, they did not believe Mexican citizens were equal to other U. S. citizens and consequently postponed granting this right and, "despite the Treaty's provision for citizenship, citizenship rights were abridged throughout the Southwest through limitations placed on voting rights and segregation in public accommodations and schooling," (Spring, 2010, p. 88).

The construct of segregation in public accommodations and schools has been perpetuated in every step of history since the end of hostilities between the United States and Mexico in 1848. In 1930, in the community of Lemon Grove California, parents took issue with the local school board and the manner in which their children were being educated and/or separated.

As in most communities in California, the population was segregated with Whites living on one side of town and Mexicans in another. Such arrangements were typical and necessary as Mexican labor was needed to work in the various production of fruits and vegetables but it was not acceptable to live on the same streets or neighborhoods.

In 1930, the school board of Lemon Grove California, decided to remove the Mexican children from the main school and house them in a barn-like structure nearby. The ostensive reason given was to teach them English until they could understand enough to transfer to the real school house. Parents noticed that the desks were ill repaired, the walls were unpainted and books outdated. They felt that anytime spent in a school such as that was a waste of time and certainly not a good education.

The school board made the decision to move the Mexican students without informing the parents. They did not count on the parents holding meetings to discuss the matter towards a course of action against this unconscionable act. When the parents decided to keep their children at home and not send them to the inferior school, the school board relented after the Superior Court of San Diego County ruled that it violated the state's Education Code (Madrid, 2008).

Mexican Americans continued to experience segregation; this time in Ontario, California in 1945. Parents there wanted to move their children from a segregated Mexican school but were denied by the school board based on the same notion that it was in "their" best interest to remain in these separate schools until they could "learn" English. A U.S. District Court ruled in favor of the parents because segregating their children from those that spoke English deprived them the ability to learn that language.

A few years later in 1954, the decision of Brown v. Board of Education "of Topeka [heard by the Supreme Court] overturned the separate but equal doctrine by arguing that segregated education was inherently unequal" (Spring, 2010, p.65). This particular case is often highlighted as pivotal in abating segregation of African American students in public schools but, the previous cases involving Mexican students helped to set a legal precedent.

Because education in public schools are commonly viewed as the way to attain a better life through increased opportunities and income, they are key and a necessity to children of Mexican Americans and other immigrants whose first language is Spanish. In the mid 1980's until the late 1990's, a series of controversial propositions were introduced and voted upon that demonstrated the disdain towards the Spanish speaking population in California. The following propositions are discussed as a way to demonstrate how the treatment of Mexican American and English Language Learners continued to play a part in the politics of education and economic attainment of this particular population group.

1986: PROPOSITION 63—ENGLISH ONLY INITIATIVE

This proposition or more specifically, *English is the Official Language of California Amendment*, declared English as the official language in California. It directs the California State Legislature to "preserve the role of English as the state's common language . . .[and] prohibits the Legislature from passing laws which diminish or ignore the role of English as the state's common language," (www.ballotpedia.org).

As official as the amendment reads, many Mexican American and immigrant group see saw this as a veiled attempt to silence the usage of their native languages while learning English. In the case of California, that language would be *Spanish* as it is the dominant language spoken by the majority minority, although several other languages were affected. It was also believed to be an attempt to stifle the cultural nuances and norms of the Mexican American in California since it is such a common occurrence in daily life. Overall, it was considered a mean-spirited attack on "those people", a commonly used term meaning immigrant or alien. Perhaps, it was a revisit to the overarching theme of the "Mexican Problem" spurred on by the Mexican American War?

1994: PROPOSITION 187—SAVE OUR STATE INITIATIVE (SOS)

This proposition was entitled, Save Our State, as it was intended to save the state from the numerous "illegal aliens" or undocumented immigrants that were jeopardizing the "American-ness" of the state. Proponents of this amendment believed this population group was costing the state of California too much money in services such as health care and public education. It was used by Governor Pete Wilson as a political rally point in his bid for re-election. Although the amendment succeeded, it was later challenged and found unconstitutional by a federal district court (www.ballotpedia.org).

1996: PROPOSITION 209—CALIFORNIA CIVIL RIGHTS INITIATIVE

This amendment to the state constitution was intended to prohibit state governmental institutions from considering race, sex, or ethnicity, in public employment, public contracting, and public education. It was modeled after the Civil Rights Act of 1964. As in other propositions of this era, it was meant to address the seemingly advantageous benefits of Affirmative Action. In this area of focus from proponents, minorities had an unfair advantage in attainment of jobs in state agencies and university admissions. Although the Civil Rights Act was intended to reverse the barriers and discrimination experienced by minorities while attempting to get out of poverty through employment and education, this was not acceptable to the White majority who felt their civil rights were violated (www.ballotpedia.org).

1998: PROPOSITION 227—BILINGUAL EDUCATION

This amendment essentially ended Bilingual Education in California as it was intended to work in the education of English Language Learners. Instead of using the mother tongue of the student while learning the mainstream language of English, students were given one year of instruction in the English language. The goal was to mainstream or place the student in a regular classroom as soon as possible. Opponents of the amendment saw it as an attack once again on language minority students and in the case of California; Spanish, in particular. Years of research by proponents of Bilingual Education demonstrated that students learn school curriculum and the second language when they are able to use their native language as a foundation. It not only provided a sense of empowerment by allowing them to use their language but, it helped in the deep critical thinking involved with attaining comprehension of long term concepts or knowledge. The fluency in English comes gradually with the use of both languages to support and facilitate language learning while not allowing the student to fall behind in academics. Of course, those that advocated for this amendment were not versed or knowledgeable in educational research that supported this point of view. Their main thrust for this initiative was for students to learn English as soon as possible because it was the official language of the state (www.languagepolicy.net).

Over the next few decades, bilingual education was changed to multilingual education and eventually to the more politically accepted term of dual language immersion or two-way immersion. It is a method of instruction that uses two languages while teaching academic content in elementary public schools. The first called 90:10 "refers to the amount of instructional time spent using the target or non English language in kindergarten" and the second number is the time spent using English. This is adjusted as the child moves on up the grades to where by sixth grade, they are receiving instruction in English 90 percent of the time. The second method is called 50:50 whereby the language usage is equal in emphasis through out the day or over the days each week. The first program method which devotes a ratio of 90:10 in kindergarten and eventually 50:50 in grades 4-6 is known to be the most effective (http://www.cde.ca.gov/sp/el/ip/faq.asp).

LATEST DEVELOPMENT AGAINST ENGLISH LANGUAGE LEARNERS

Recently, Ron Unz, the sponsor of Proposition 227 or more commonly advertised as "English for the Children" that was passed in 1998, has announced that he is running for the 2016 senate seat in California in order to defeat an initiative that will dismantle "his" proposition when it comes through the senate. It is a bipartisan amendment that acknowledges the benefit of Dual Immersion as a method of learning a second language while maintaining a high level of academic achievement. Mr. Unz feels that his proposition was an effective way for English to be mastered by students contrary to what research states.

CALIFORNIA PUBLIC SCHOOLS, LATINO/A STUDENTS NOW COMPRISE THE MAJORITY MINORITY

The number of minority students affected by these previous amendments to the constitution of the State of California and now with Mr. Unz as he considers stepping into the political arena once again in an attempt to subdue bipartisan efforts to change laws that are harmful to speakers of languages other than English and contrary to what is stated in the research is shown in the following table (www.cde.ca.gov).

One has to imagine what the true motives are for Mr. Unz to return to the political arena in defense of previous propositions that have been harmful to English Language Learners and at a time when Dual Immersion is being advocated as a preferred method of teaching academic content to students who have difficulty learning in English. Also, now that they are the majority minority and the Local Control Funding Formulas (LCFF) are in place to increase parent participation and student success. One has to believe that when a solution that works for other children is brought to the forefront of education, it must be challenged as is the case with Mr. Unz and his political agenda.

English Language Learners

English learners make up a significant portion of California public school students: The 1,392,263 English learners constitute 22.3 percent of the total enrollment in California public schools. A total of 2,672,128 students (English Learners and Fluent English Proficient) speak a language other than English in their homes. This number represents about 42.9 percent of the state's public school enrollment. Spanish (87.7%) is the language most spoken by this population group with 12.3 percent speaking a language other than English (www.cde.ca.gov).

The Schools and the Educational System

The amount of students that are labeled as Latino/a in California is staggering in comparison to other minority groups. There is no doubt that this population group is the majority minority once and for all. As the years pass since the attainment of this statistical status, public schools and the educational system in general from K-16 needs to ask itself if it is serving this population adequately? The economic future and stability of this state depends on a well educated and gainfully employed population. What has worked and what more needs to be done in order to meet this task?

In California the recent changes to the way school finances are delegated to the individual school districts is a step in the right direction. Through Local Control Funding Formulas

Table 1 Ethnic Distribution of Public School Students: 2014–15

Ethnicity	Number of students	Percentage
Hispanic or Latino	3,344,431	53.25%
Pacific Islander	31,513	0.53%
White not Hispanic	1,531,088	25.00%
Two or More Races Not Hispanic	175,700	2.68%

(LCFF), separate funding streams for oversight activities and instructional programs are provided after consultation with teachers, administrators and parents of the school district. Allowing parents to have input on what is provided for their children in public schools puts parents at the forefront of decision making. It is imperative for them to actively participate and not be afraid to be heard as is often the common theme among Latino/a parents or immigrant parents (www.cde.ca.gov).

Schools need to be a place where students want to attend because the learning is exciting, challenging, and a language difference is seen as an attribute and not a deficit as it is still currently perceived by society. The school buildings and grounds need to reflect an aura that the students who attend there are valued and worthy of a clean, well-equipped learning environment. The schools should have resources and equipment that match those found in all middle or upper class schools where parents demand such things because they experienced the same when they attended public schools and succeeded in society.

Current Movements

Black Lives Matter is a movement created by Millennials and Baby Boomers after a series of deaths at the hands of law enforcement. In all cases, the deaths were African American youth or men and the reason for use of deadly force varied but the outcome was the same: death. The movement has grown throughout the United States through blogs, tweets, Instagram, and any/all other social media outlets. There is a backlash and counter movement titled "All Lives Matter" which points out the obvious; that all lives matter but, also sends a message that diminishes the importance of minority treatment by law enforcement. For too many in our society, when other people's children find themselves in circumstances beyond their control, our current society tends to diminish or discount the experience. This same attitude is carried over to the children of immigrants or "Dreamers" who through no choice of their own were brought to this country at a young age and therefore, were not citizens of this country. The Dream Act or Development, Relief, and Education for Alien Minors is meant to offer a multi- phase process for undocumented immigrants to obtain permanent residency (Kim, 2013).

The first test in the process toward citizenship is for the Dreamers to determine the following: 1) Did they come to the United States when they were 16 years or younger, and 2) Have they lived here for five years or more? Second, have they earned a high school diploma or equivalent or have they been admitted to a college or university in the United States and making good progress towards a degree?

The next stage and one that leads to full legal status as a citizen is for the student to maintain a good moral character by not breaking any laws etc. Also, they must meet one of three requirements: a two year vocational or college degree, completion of two years in a higher degree program or service in the armed forces for two years and be honorably discharged (Kim, 2013).

The general public must be educated on the step process mentioned above so as to inform them of the main reason for the DREAM Act. That is, to create law-abiding, educated, and gainfully employed individuals that contribute to society in ways that their talents can demonstrate. The public must be asked to look beyond the hateful rhetoric of immigration and such protests as "make them go to the back of the line" or "make them go back to where they came from", in order to see that these Latino students are already here and are more Americanized and acculturated than other immigrants. They have a lot to offer and gain by being allowed to attend college or enlist in the military.

CONCLUSION

Given the preponderance of evidence for the need to educate any/all children of Mexican American and immigrant families, there are still segments of our society that complain that immigrant children are receiving preferential treatment. This is strikingly more prevalent in states where the Latino/a Spanish speaking communities exist.

There needs to be a movement similar to Black Lives Matter that will put out the information necessary to inform the public and especially those who would listen to the cause of the Latino/a immigrant experience. It is predicted that by the mid Twenty First Century, Latinos will make up nearly 30 percent or 127 million of the US population. A message needs to be developed, marketed, and repeated often as to the contribution this population group gives to the social and economic well being of this country. The public schools, colleges and universities should carry this message throughout its mission statement as it recruits and educates students. As a country that was founded on diversity, we need to care about the lives of people that live in our country, all people, all Latinos/as.

Atl
Water

CHAPTER 9

CHICANA-LATINA LITERATURE: LIFE AND EXPERIENCES

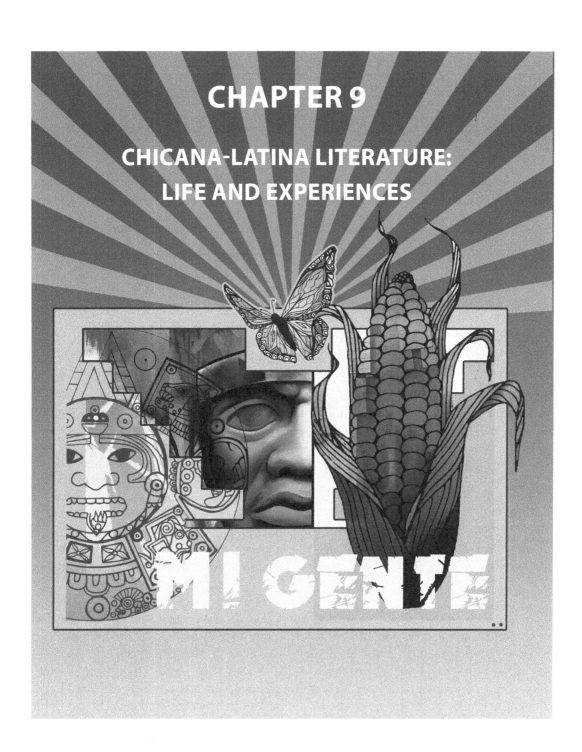

The true story of *La Raza* requires an examination and understanding of the world, reality, and existence as seen through the perception of women. Mothers, grandmothers, and great-grandmothers are not only *life-givers* but *life-teachers*. Chicana-Latina literature is having a profound impact on the understanding of culture, family, and community. The following are essays of seven unique women who share their profound insights. The first two literary pieces are examples of creative writing. The remaining essays are autobiographical stories.

Linda Ramos is an English professor. Her interests focus on creative writing. Following is the story of life as seen through the eyes of a little girl. The title is *Mother*.

She dragged me by my arm and off of my red bike. She wanted to comb my hair. My head hurt, as she pulled my hair into a pony-tail on the terrace. Sammy clicked his heels as he walked toward us. "Tell your kids to keep their hands to themselves. I have a lot of expensive equipment here," said Sammy, Mother's jazz musician boyfriend. We'd been staying at his house for a few weeks.

Mother took a deep drag from her cigarette and looked to the sky. "But they're just kids, Sammy. Why don't you tell Mrs. Sanchez to keep a closer watch on them?" Mrs. Sanchez was Sammy's maid and she annoyed me.

"You know what, little kids irritate me. They're in the way. I have to keep my guard up whenever they're around. I can't relax. That's why I've never had kids. Remember, they're your kids, not mine."

"Sammy, please, don't get so upset."

I knew Mother cared about Sammy more than Brother and me. He bought her lots of jewelry and clothes and I knew she'd soon get rid of Brother and me. The next morning, when I went downstairs, Abuelita was in the kitchen wearing her green coat and had on a scarf that I'd given her for her birthday. I grabbed her smooth, cool hands. They weren't sweaty and rough, like Mrs. Sanchez's hands.

On the way to Fresno, from San Jose, I counted the trees so that I'd know how many trees to count to get back to Mother. I hoped that Mother would miss and need me. I lost count. I didn't know where Fresno was, and I thought that it was just a few miles from Mother so that I could still see her every day. The trip seemed to take forever. I saw big farms that smelled like strong pee. I saw men, women and children cutting grapes on a farm that we passed and some families picking oranges on other farms. There was one lady on a ladder near an orange tree with a red bandana on. Her face reminded me of Mother. Her baby was sitting near the ladder. What if the mother's ladder fell on the baby, I thought. Was it okay to take the baby to work like that? After a few days, I started missing Mother reading to me and playing games before bed. Maybe she'd come to live with us, I thought. I didn't see Mother for a very long time. Brother and I put one of her pictures by our beds. Brother cried at night and soon got sick with a fever and cough. I got a knotted feeling in my throat every time that I looked at Mother's picture, but I decided that I'd be a big girl. Mother didn't miss me, so I decided to not miss her. She wanted to be with Sammy.

Abuelita's house was cozy. Abuelito kept it warm. He built a wooden bunk bed for Brother and me with a ladder so that Brother could get to the top bunk; but Brother's legs were too short, and Abuelito had to pick him up and place him on his bunk, since he couldn't climb there. Abuelito put pillows all around Brother so that he wouldn't fall off.

"Pelon, you must keep your guns, holsters and toys under the bottom bunk bed in your toy box, *mijo*," said Abuelito while stroking Brother's hair. Brother clapped and pinched Abuelito's cheeks and giggled. He loved Abuelito. Abuelito called Brother "Pelon" because Brother had a bald head when he was born and for a very long time after.

"Juan, *dejalo*. He'll be okay," said Abuelita. She took Brother from Abuelito's arms and wiped some sticky chocolate off of his chin.

Abuelito took out a Howdy Doody doll from under his pillow and gave it to Brother. Howdy Doody was Brother's favorite toy. He squealed with joy. I looked at them. I think Abuelito thought that I felt left out. He said that he had something extra special for me. He took out a big box. I tore it open. There were new crayons, paper dolls, drawing paper and lots of little books. Abuelito said that I would one day grow up to be a teacher and I had to be a good reader. I ran and kissed his red cheek and then went to Abuelita and showed her my treasure box. I put my head on her chest and she sang to me. Everything was good here. Everything. But one day, Brother got sicker. His little body got thin and weak. His legs gave out when he wanted to walk. He had a fever that Abuelita had a hard time controlling with *ruda* and *verbena*. He didn't like the teas and would spit them

out. She put towels, which had been soaked in cool water, on his forehead. One day when we woke up early, we found him on the floor, weeping. He couldn't walk. Dr. Mau came to the house. He said Brother had polio. Pelon couldn't even crawl and Abuelito had to carry him. Abuelita said not to worry that she would pray to her saints and Brother would get well. She gave him more teas to drink. He cried for Mother. He carried a small picture of her. Mother said she couldn't come, but she'd try to come soon.

Abuelita's house was near the farm where Abuelito worked. He said that in Fresno there weren't many jobs. He regretted having to leave his job at Almaden Winery. This house was not large like their house in San Jose. It had only three rooms, no furnace, and no indoor toilet. I'd not seen a house with no toilet. The farmer provided only a public outhouse toilet, several yards from our house. It was made out of wood. The wooden toilet was in a little house that smelled like chemicals when the door was opened. The hole to sit on was large and I was afraid of falling in. The hole looked very deep and it was filled with awful stuff. I didn't want any of that on my skin, if I fell in there, I thought. I was afraid to fall, so Abuelita went with me and held my hands, as I sat in that shack. Brother refused to go to the outhouse so Abuelito bought him a traveling urinal to use.

"Juan, it's getting too dangerous for the kids to use that outhouse. There are too many men around during this season," Abuelita said to Abuelito. I jumped on Abuelito's overstuffed chair and watched my grandparents as they talked. He went over to Abuelita and put his arm around her shoulders. Brownie, our dog, seemed interested too and sat on the floor looking at my Abuelito talk.

Abuelito said, "I never thought that I'd have to live like this again. We've not lived in a bathroomless house in decades. I'm happy that you're staying with us, *mija*. You bring much joy to your Abuelita's heart, and to mine, too." I knew that he was telling the truth.

I looked around the house. I wanted to make my grandparents happy. They'd made me happy and I wanted to help them. All the walls were empty. All their paintings were in storage in San Jose. I decided that I would help Abuelita decorate the house. When Mother visited I would ask her to take us shopping to buy some new curtains and new furniture. Abuelita would like to have a big four-poster bed like she had in San Jose. I'd ask Mother to buy her one. She'd be coming to see us soon and I would have Abuelito make a list for me and send it to her so that she would know what Abuelita needed. I knew that Sammy would buy her whatever she wanted.

I slept in the same room with my grandparents and ate Abuelita's homemade food: she was always at home, unlike Mother. She taught me how to can peaches and make *camotes con leche* with sugar. My box of books, dolls and toys were under my bed. Before bed, she filled an aluminum tub with warm water that she heated on the stove for baths. There was no built-in tub, nor closets.

We planted rose bushes and a vegetable garden. Lita taught me how to make little rows in the dirt and water the dirt to keep it moist. She taught me how to start the plants in little miniature tubs. When they were a few inches tall, we transplanted them into the soil. We watered the soft soil and soon each plant started to thrive. Abuelita kept a compost pile nearby that she used to fertilize the plants. Soon we had tomatoes, chilies, lettuce, peppers, squash and big pumpkins. When the pumpkins were ripe Abuelita made *empanadas de calabaza*; and we roasted the pumpkin seeds. She kept the seeds near Abuelito's kerosene lamp where he read *La Opinion* and Alan Kardec's metaphysical books in the evenings. He liked to munch on the pumpkin seeds while he devoured as much reading as possible before it was too dark to see, since there was no electricity. He said that the seeds contained *minerales* and that they helped him to see better. He said that since he'd been eating them he didn't need to wear his glasses.

Sometimes Abuelita prepared *menudo*. She let me put the cut-up *menudo* and hominy in a big pot that she boiled like a soup on weekends and served with cut up onions, *limon* and *oregano* or *cilantro*; and we made homemade corn tortillas from *asa arina*. The tortillas were thick and could be slit open after they were done cooking on the *comal*. We drizzled melted butter on them and rolled them up and dipped them in the beans or *menudo*.

Grandma planted a rose garden near the front of the house. When they grew and blossomed there were different-colored roses. One of my favorites was a large yellow bloom and a bush of wild roses called *rosa de castilla* that the neighbors borrowed when their babies had colic, gases, or constipation. Abuelita said that the modern mothers didn't want to spend time breastfeeding their babies and that's why they got sick. She said she had nine children and she breastfed them all and there was no excuse for using the bottle. She said that cow's milk was for calves and that mother's milk was for babies. When the mothers near our house came to Abuelita for advice for colic, she gave them the *rosa de castilla* and told them to boil it with *nuez moscada*, or sometimes she gave them *manzanilla*. When the mothers whined that they couldn't make enough milk to feed their babies, Abuelita combined *hinojo* and *cardon,* in tea form, to increase their milk supply. One day a neighbor brought her baby girl over. She had large blisters on her lips, inside her mouth and on her face. The blisters had started to spread to her hands and arms. The doctor had told her it was impetigo. Abuelita ground some *mirra*. The baby's problem was gone in two days. The mother told Abuelita that the doctor was amazed.

Abuelita kept us busy and she gave me lots of storybooks in Spanish that she had from her childhood. There was a picture book that showed different objects with the Spanish and English names on the side of the pictures. Brother and I were writing our own book to send to Mother. Brother and I drew pictures and colored them. We drew a picture on ten sheets of paper. Each picture was different. In the evening, Abuelito wrote a sentence on the bottom of the picture. One picture was a drawing of Brother and I cutting peaches off of the peach tree and another picture was of Abuelita making empanadas with the peaches that we had picked. We drew a picture of Brownie, Abuelito's dog, with Brother and his holster. "Ninos, when we finish, we'll send this to your Mother in this envelope.

It'll be a nice surprise for her. She'll love it. *Le va gustar muchisimo,*" Abuelito said. I hoped that she would. On the last page of our book, we drew a picture of Mother holding my hand and Brother's hand. The sun was in the background surrounded by a blue sky. She had a big smile on her face. I hoped that Mother would smile when she saw that last picture.

One day I sat in the front room of the house near the corner where there was black mold and moldy odor, and I heard Brownie barking madly. I looked out of the window and saw a yellow cab and a lady dressed in fancy clothes giving the driver some money. She had red heels on and a red two-piece business suit. This lady had blond hair and she did not look like anyone that lived around our house. I took a closer look. It was Mother. I was surprised by her new hair color. She looked like a movie star. I ran out to meet her.

The first thing Mother said was, "How can you stand it here? It's such a hick town!" She walked into a small hole and one of her high heels broke off. She held on to me so that she wouldn't fall. "Oh, darn," she said. Brownie kept barking, as she walked near our house. She said, "Shut up, shut up. You pesky little runt." She came in the house and hugged Abuelita.

Mother brought many gifts wrapped in rainbow-colored metallic paper and large ribbons. She said that she couldn't sleep nor have peace of mind with Brother and me in Fresno and Brother being sick. What I thought was that she and Sammy had a fight because I didn't think she cared about

Brother and me much. Maybe she didn't like sick children, like Brother, or children who couldn't talk very well, like me. Or maybe she felt guilty. We had fun while she was there. She and I spent hours cutting and dressing paper dolls, reading, coloring and playing ball. She'd wanted to be a dress designer when she was younger and she taught me how to make clothes for the paper dolls and she taught me how to color them and make little paper tabs so that they would stay on the doll. I made a coat with fur for one of the dolls and boots with fur that matched the coat along with a matching hat. I felt like I was living happily ever after. Mother was fun and relaxed. After a while, I felt like she loved us. She didn't hug me and she didn't tell me that she loved me, but I just hoped that she did. She didn't hug me or Brother. Hugging didn't come easy to Mother. Brother became healthier, while Mother was with us.

Mother and I took walks. The farm-workers, who'd left their wives and families in their country, whistled at Mother when we passed by. She hated it and I hated it. It made me feel sick. She looked out of place in her calf-length Capris and cashmere sweater. The women at the store, who were Mother's age, wore ragged housedresses. They had ragged rollers and smelled of cooking oil or lard. They had long dirty uneven fingernails and looked like they'd never heard of makeup. Mother looked liked she'd walked out of a fashion magazine. I felt proud of Mother. I knew the other women envied her and the men wanted to get close to her. I wanted to be like Mother, but I wasn't beautiful like her, I thought. Mother was special and I was not.

She brought Brother and me boxes of new clothes that she wanted to put away in a closet. But there weren't any closets. Soon she grew anxious and frustrated and dumped the clothes on the floor.

"Ay, mama. How do you stand it here?" Abuelita didn't say anything. "I need to change," Mother said. She went to the back of the house and came out wearing black Capri pants that ended near her knees and a pink angora sweater with buttons in the back and open-toed heels that matched her sweater. She complained about everything, no phone, no toilet, no Sammy. She wanted a shower every day, which was impossible. There was no shower and no bathtub and she didn't want to stay. I knew she missed Sammy. I knew that she wanted to be with Sammy more than with us. I wanted Mother to love Brother and me more. I wanted her to love us more than Sammy. Sammy was a stranger. She'd known us longer than him. Why did she want to be with him? I didn't understand. I thought mothers should stay with their children. I thought mothers would care about their children. She looked at his picture constantly. She looked at Brother on his bike struggling with the pedals and then she looked at me. We looked at Mother, with tears in our eyes. She left.

Sylvia Savala is a college professor and artist. Her specialty is painting and creative writing. This essay is a unique insight into the life of a little girl living in the *barrio*. It is titled *See How Vanilla Runs*.

There were *50–50s*, fudge bars, ice cream sandwiches, boxes filled with Abazabas wrapped in black and white wrappers, and Sugar Daddys that lasted for hours. On the counter were *dulces de leche y canela*, whose soft morsels of sweet cinnamon melted in my mouth, and next to them was my favorite *dulces de calavasa* that was made with sweet pumpkin.

But it was the sawdust-scent of pine that caught my attention when I entered. I pushed the sawdust side to side in an ice skating motion, watching it gather into long fluffy piles. Nana always had sawdust on the floor because it helped keep it clean. When she sprinkled it, it fell into a halo just like the feed did when she fed the chickens. I watched some gather in broods, as others rushed to her cackling all the while.

And like the chickens, people gathered at Nana's grocery store, The Pinedale Food Basket. She greeted her customers with a smile and enthusiasm. Customers like La Sra. Diaz came to her to cure stomach and earaches, Mr. Gonzalez came to her to ask how to write a check, La Sra. Martinez came to learn how to pay her electric bill, and Yolanda, a single mother, wanted to know how to get her son out of bed and on to school. She also wanted to know how to sew a hem. Nana gave them the information they needed; she knew just about everything.

There were, at that time, four other little grocery stores like Nana's in Pinedale, where the customer was recognized as a friend. All but one store remains. Now that I no longer live there, I shop at the local SHOP CO where I've been buying groceries for more than twenty years, and I've yet to be addressed by my name. I've sadly learned not to expect special treatment. I'm grateful to get out without having to wait in a long line.

I still remember Nana sitting on a crate behind the counter, slightly stooped over, reading the newspaper. She wore her silver hair in a bob that accentuated her jaw line and a blue industrial apron folded and tied up to her waist.

"Hi Nan-a-a-a," I called out.

"*Ay, Hija, c-o-o-mo estas?*"

"Good, Nana." I spoke English to Nana because I was forgetting how to speak Spanish. Daddy ordered Mama not to speak Spanish to us because he was afraid we'd end up speaking broken English like her. It shamed Daddy.

"*Quieres una soda, Hija?*" The sodas were to the right. I stopped in front of the three glass doors filled with rows of small green bottles of Coca Cola, A&W Root Beer, and *Calandra* orange and strawberry sodas.

"Maybe you want a small cherry pie or *unos de esos puerquitos?*"

I smiled at Nana, and then looked over to the pastries shaped like little pigs whose flavor I would later associate with gingerbread men.

"Nana, Mama wants cilantro, baking powder, cottage cheese, and a can of peaches." She slowly got up, passing the big gunnysacks filled with *frijoles, arroz*, and *cebollas*. Nana bought large amount of beans, rice and onions; they were the staples of her customers.

As she took the items to the counter, I cruised to the silver ice cream box, peeked at the *helados* and fudge bars but decided on the fancy Neapolitan ice cream sandwich with its three layers of vanilla, strawberry, and chocolate. I then sat on the crate next to the bubble gum machine, which was perched at the doorway and began tearing off the wrapper.

"How's your mama and your brother?" and before I could answer, she asked, "How did you do in school today, *Hija*?" School was very important to Nana, who had successfully encouraged some of her children to attend the nearby university.

No sooner had I taken a bite of the backside of the sandwich when I heard the screen door open. It was La Sra. Martinez, wearing an apron cut from a flour sack with an image of a man playing a guitar, singing to a beautiful woman with long black braids. It reminded me of one of the Mexican movies that I had seen with Mama: the handsome Pedro Infante with his big sombrero sang ballads to his one and only love. The girl wore a *rebozo* with yellow and purples that curved like a frown. I then noticed the handiwork on the apron and how each stitch led to another.

La Sra Martinez said, "Ay, my little one has an earache so I couldn't send her to school."

"*Mira,* smash a little bit of garlic, mix it with a teaspoon of warm olive oil and put it in her ear with a piece of *algodon*," Nana said. None of this was news to me. Mama had learned all this from her mother who in turn had learned it from hers. Mama knew ways to rid us of our fevers, stomachaches, and earaches, making fewer visits to Dr. Bradley.

Nana listened carefully, tilting her head slightly to the right. I took tiny bites from the sandwich, creating corrugated edges. I wondered all the while how she managed to listen to so many problems. I then looked up towards the back of the store where there was a big Coca-Cola sign with a girl with blonde hair. She looked like my friend Kathy Carter, who lived in a quiet, blue and white house. Our house had red and orange curtains, and Mama played South American music (the latest craze) on her hi-fi that yelled out the windows like a crazy woman. The brown and gold netting that covered the speaker couldn't even muffle it.

But Kathy had beautiful golden waves like Rapunzel. I watched it ripple down the back of the seat as I rode the bus, thinking all the while how much it looked like my doll's hair. I liked mine; black and straight hair, nothing like hers. I turned and looked at my reflection in the glass refrigerator doors, smoothing my hair down, feeling the silky strands in the curve of my hand. I checked to make sure my favorite clip with the pink rose was in place and adjusted my matching neck scarf just a tad. I thought I looked good.

My fingers pressed the chocolaty dough together, squishing the vanilla out. Maybe I did it too hard; the two sides of the sandwich collapsed. Nana was visiting with La Sra. Martinez; I sat alone with my legs dangling under the crate, watching vanilla melt down my hand.

Sallie Perez Saiz is a professor of English. In addition to creative writing, she is involved in literary journalism covering U.S.–Mexican border issues including immigrant rights. The following essay is the story relating to her identity as a Chicana. Her essay is, *What's in a Word*.

Chicano Power . . . Chicana . . . meant being on the outside and unified at the same time. I look back as a young girl and remember my parents entrusting our family with the words Chicano Power, creating a gift, a piece of American history. Chicano Power had many deviations, profane associations, outlaw connotations, and spiritual revelations—but to me it was simple.

I was three years old when my family began to actively support Cesar Chavez and the United Farm workers Union. Weekends I woke to the smell of *chorizo* and eggs, and *frijoles* as my mother prepared burritos for my father, two brothers, four sisters, and me. Sleepy-eyed, I walked into the kitchen and spotted my mother leaning over the counter filling the tortilla, rolling it then wrapping it in foil for a trip to Del Rey, Sanger, or Parlier. Some days, while wedging our bodies into the station wagon, we went further to Tulare, Delano, Corcoran, Riverdale, Lindsey, Porterville, and, much later, San Francisco. Memories run together of people marching, intertwining like the knarled vines of sticky sweet grapes that permeated my life.

Once, on a hot day in March, several hundred farmworkers marched into downtown Fresno, tired and hungry, a week into their three-hundred-mile trek from Delano to Sacramento. Early the next day, priests blessed the marchers, and the pilgrimage pressed on from the Azteca Theatre. Joining the march, my parents proceeded the short distance from Fresno to Madera, following Cesar's jet black hair, the red UFW AFL-CIO flag with the black eagle, and the *virgen* as she wafted forward overhead draped in her green *reboza*. Farmworkers, visible against the grape vineyards lining the Golden State Highway, walked the miles and miles of pavement and dirt roads north. Beautiful voices singing *corridos* floated by, stirred up the dust, rose and fell to the beat of raised fist and thudding feet, as the marchers propelled themselves forward. The weary occasionally stopped to sit and rest on the dirt road, next to nearby fields. My grandfather drove alongside the marchers, frequently dropping behind, while my siblings and I hung our heads out the window, watching the stream of traffic slow and listening to catcalls hovering in the air.

Two weeks later, I sat in the backseat of our station wagon as we drove to meet the marchers at the Capitol rally. The single-file line had grown, and I found myself absorbed by the sea of bodies. Familiar brown faces resting under the tall trees looked out of place against the opulent buildings. My dad hoisted me on top of his shoulders. I steadied myself, overlooking the mass of people as everyone gathered around Cesar.

Over the years, we met out of town at small parks. Organizing ourselves in a line behind Cesar, we walked through the countryside or the town waving our UFW flags singing and chanting *"Huelga,"* or *"Viva La Causa"* to support the boycott of non-union grapes or lettuce. The red flags whipped back and forth from the shifting of our bodies as we marched forward. The black eagle floated in the dry heat gaining momentum at each fork in the road. One foot, then the other, I methodically marched in a single-file line walking along the dusty roads, feeling the heat and particles of dirt penetrating my young skin. Voices, echoing from the mass of people in Sacramento and into the present, answered Cesar and Dolores Huerta's call, *"Que Viva la Causa."*

The crowd responded, *"Viva."*

And again, *"Viva la Huelga!"*

The crowd roared *"Viva!"* then erupted into, *"Viva la Huelga!"*

Until one day I heard my own voice rising to meet the other voices when I shouted, *"Viva la Huelga!"*

At the end of the march, when we gathered around Cesar, he spoke out against the lack of toilettes, water, and adequate pay for farmworkers, and strongly opposed farmers who crop-dusted their fields while workers were in the fields picking the crops. He championed the value of hard work, the contribution of farmworkers for communities across the world, and the perseverance of faith to rise up out of the daily tasks of one's life to continue *la huelga* for basic human rights. Cesar's voice soared over us, *"Si se puede,"* to continue the strike on packing sheds or big growers who weren't negotiating with the union. Demanding the strike on stores buying non-union grapes, non-union fruits, and non-union vegetables, *el gritó, "Huelga!"*

The crowd began to clap their hands, answering his call, *"Si se puede!"* striking the echo up with their feet, thundering, *"Huelga. Huelga. Huelga."*

Afterwards, sitting out on the grass in the laps of Esther, Amelia, or Cecilia, who were college students—looking around at all those in my life I looked up to . . . my parents, sisters, brothers, friends, and leaders of the community was a moment of unity, a feeling of completeness. I made my way to the tables holding memorabilia, picking up the brown-raised-hand in the shape of a fist, turning it around and gazing at this small wooden carving. Next, I picked up little patches that read Chicano Power, reminiscing about the day and these small mementoes of the *movimiento*. After I thought about it for a long time, I finally asked my mother if I could purchase the brown fist.

We made many trips during those years and participated in many pickets, following the vision of a better tomorrow. On the drives home it usually turned dark before we reached home, but I never fell asleep. I kept watch over my father, tired at the wheel. I sat up in the rear of our station wagon, looking out over the fields of vegetables and fruits, silent, as my father drove, glancing at my mother, my four sisters, and my two brothers as they slept. When we drove into Fresno, I breathed a sigh of relief, glad we were home safe, then lay down to pretend that I was asleep. I heard everyone waking, talking, leaving toward the house, then felt my father's arms around me, picking me up to carry me in and felt my mother kiss me before she pulled the covers up over me as I dropped off to sleep—smiling.

In the summer of seventh grade, my mother, younger sister, younger brother, and I moved to Stanford where my mother attended graduate school. My father and my other siblings stayed in Fresno. We were gone for two years, but on the weekends my father either drove up to see us or we came home. I waited for those weekends when we returned home as we rounded the bend towards the 99, dropping into the valley. Through my open window, the heat blasted my face with the sweet stench of earth mixed with grapes, stabilizing my breathing, and I involuntarily relaxed my body.

My consciousness continued to evolve; with my mother at Stanford, I was now the eldest child, with no sisters or brother to watch over me. But being the eldest child now brought many responsibilities as I helped my mother by watching over my younger siblings. For the first time in my life I had a room to myself. I set up a shelf on the wall, and on it I put my brown fist next to the carving I had made that read, Earth, Wind, and Fire, and another one that read *Jefe* (Chief), who was my horse. We had friends from different countries—other families that were living away from their cultures, apart from their families. I missed my family, especially my Grandma-Mother. At school, where I was bused to Los Altos Hills, there were only two other Chicanos; they were brother and sister; the majority of the students were either white or black. I had trouble figuring out where I fit in. I missed being in the midst of *mi cultura*, hearing the sounds of the marches. It was at these times that I often picked up the carving of the hand to run my fingers over the fist made out of wood, daydreaming about teenage dreams, my friends, and my home.

I began to notice the division among the students and the racist remarks directed at the black students. At first when things were said about others I remained quiet, especially when one of the white students I knew would say that so-and-so was a "nigger." In their eyes, I guess they must have felt comfortable blurting out something like that, though I didn't understand why. But slowly the urge to rise up was beginning to formulate in my stomach until I uttered, "Hey, don't talk like that. And, definitely, not in front of me."

The response was, "Well, what's it to you? We're not talking about you." But, I felt sure, if that was the way they felt about the black kids then they must've felt the same about the Mexican kids. I began to feel that some of these biased feelings were directed at me. Remarks intended to make me feel included, "Oh, but you're different, you're not like the others," drove me away even further.

I thought *but, who are the others?* and said, "Oh, you mean like my sisters and brothers, or my grandparents?" as I looked into their eyes.

This battle to retain my identity began to consume me. I began to doodle on one of my school folders, Chicano Power. One day in the ninth grade, a white girl named Patty leaned over and asked, "What's *that* supposed to mean?"

I tensed up and stated, "It means *like* Brown Power."

She sneered, "Well that's stupid!"

It was at this time that my sense of myself as an outsider came into better focus, the fact that I am a Chicana—for better or worse—caught between two worlds.

It is my own hand that I pick up to gaze at now. I think about what it represents, looking at my olive-brown skin. Below the brown surface, it represents a spirit that is very strong and has persevered through many troubled times . . . Chicana . . . Chicano Power. It has a history and when I feel the barriers that present themselves in life, I think back to the history of its origins; there is strength in the color brown. It is the color of the earth, the mother earth—and from it, we gather the strength to continue the search for an indigenous place in North American history.

Teresa Tarazi is an English professor. She also teaches Chicano-Latino Studies. As a professor, Teresa has a profound impact on her students. In the following essay she shares a pivotal experience. The title is *Chicano-Latino Studies 9.*

At Fresno State, I took Chicano-Latino Studies 9 with Dr. Martinez. He read *I Am Joaquín* with fervency and dignity. Goose bumps covered my skin with pregnant dots, each one filled with a birthing pride. Joaquin's sleeping giant awoke my every sense and I would no longer remain asleep. Listening to the pride I heard in his voice and in that poem, in my culture and heritage, lifted my head and broadened my shoulders.

As the last line left his lips, my journey began as Dr. Martinez placed the poem down and picked up his chalk, writing in large bold letters on the blackboard, "Write a poem about what it means to be Mexican." He turned around dramatically and continued, "You will read your poems in class; so make sure they are worth the ears we lend you!" After class I headed home, but those bold words hanging on the blackboard took me to another place and another time, distant but vivid and alive.

Suddenly, I was seven years old again, wearing my new blue dress with white dandelions around the collar. The first week of my third-grade year at Stevenson Elementary brought an excitement that tickled the air.

After finishing my spelling word list before smarty-pants Katie Adams, I won the coveted privilege of wiping the blackboard clean during recess. I remember standing next to my teacher's desk while joyfully smacking the erasers together, watching my powdered snowstorm swirl delightfully downward. She was correcting our spelling tests and after the last grade had been given, she set the small stack of papers at the corner of her desk, looked at me and smiled.

"You're not like other Mexicans," Mrs. Jones declared. "You're smart."

Mrs. Jones, a tall, thin redhead from Missouri, reminded me of a mule when she smiled her buck-tooth smile. This was one of those times. Her protruding bright pink gums emphasized her large coffee-stained front teeth. She patted my third-grade shoulder and continued, "After you clean the blackboard, you may have a lollipop for later." Although the word "lollipop" could arrest any child's heart, my flushed red face, hardly noticeable beneath a dark bronze summer tan, revealed an instant wound to my person, *my people, my family.*

Try as I might, I could not feel proud about what she spoke over me. Her perpetual smile became a sad commentary of deceit when she applauded Maria for her math genius or Abel's ability to draw Bugs Bunny exactly like the Saturday morning cartoon. Perhaps I was foolish to believe what she said about me was true. Perhaps it was my brown counterparts who were smart while I was the "other" Mexican.

Martinez's deadline brought me back and I obsessed with words that would make Zapata proud and Hidalgo shout a *Grito*. I considered writing about Mayan civilization, Juarez, the Aztec warrior, the word Chicano, revolution and *La Raza,* but I couldn't seem to erase Mrs. Jones's words. Again, Martinez's assignment thrust me onward. *What does it mean to be a Mexican*?

Two days later and five minutes before class on bended knee, I wrote in desperation ten little lines. The class was full. Every seat was taken, so some students stood leaning against the walls, while others were sprawled on the floor, Indian style. Professor Martinez walked in and twisted and turned his way to the front of the room. "Okay, students, let's not waste anyone's time here. Who has a deep calling to go first?" Some students shuffled about, but most stood still, trying to blend into one another so as not to be noticed. A rush of nervousness went over my body. *Don't move,* I told myself, but when he looked at me I couldn't help but smile, that was just my way. "Teresa, come on up." There were exhales of relief heard as I approached the front. Since Martinez called me up first, I knew I had to deliver, so with all the acting devices I had learned and leaned on in previous years, I read my poem.

I stood in the front center of the room. I raised my head and narrowed my eyes; my voice became strong with discontent, bordering on sneering, as I read the first sentence:

Go back to where you came from.

There was a clearing of a throat and a tremor of giggles sprinkled throughout the room. I dug in deeper for my next few lines.

You bring diseases,

Poverty,

And war.

After "war," I paused for emphasis and reflection, and then looked down at my next line. I heard someone mumble a foul word in the back row and several people moved in their seats. I don't know what came over me. Maybe it was Mrs. Jones and her words, but all of a sudden I felt a surge of anger rise up in me. I continued, but this time I looked directly into Fat Louie's eyes as I spoke one word and then changed my stare to capture Marina's gaze with another. They were the "other" Mexicans. My furrowed brow very different from my familiar smile narrowed into defiance. For a moment, I stumbled on my words as I tried to read the next line. Mrs. Jones was with me now and I was ready to indict them all, yet when I saw in Marina's eyes my own, I stumbled again. She too knew these words of accusation well, chanted over our people for generations. I regained my composure, and in that instance, I knew why I was here; so with accusation, I exploded:

You are lazy!

And dumb!

Fat Louie's ever present giggle turned into a snicker and Marina gave me the finger. In the short time, I became a traitor to my people. Even Mr. Martinez looked a little uncomfortable, not sure where I was going, but willing to see it to the end. Empowered, I continued with an even more sinister tone:

You don't even know the language.

And with a crescendo of excitement I could no longer contain, I ended with a simple couplet of redemption:

Go back to where you came from,

Yes, you—Gringo from Europe.

For a moment, the class stood silent, surrendering those words placed on them, pushing them out and giving them back, without regret or shame. In that moment of silence I emerged a new person, birthed from revolution and revolt, and I brought them with me.

Mrs. Jones was right about one thing: I am smart.

Enid Perez is a professor of Chicano-Latino Studies. She is also an attorney. In the following essay, Enid shares her life experience, *From Grape Fields to the Legal Field*.

I grew up in the small agricultural community of Del Rey, California; an unincorporated town 12 miles southeast of Fresno with a population of about 1,000 people, the majority of Mexican descent. I am the eldest of seven children; my parents were both farm workers working in the fields of the San Joaquin Valley. As a young child, I accompanied my parents to the fields and as a teenager I worked in the fields picking grapes and tomatoes to pay for my school clothes.

My experience working in the fields inspired me to become an attorney. I was 14 years old and riding in the back of a pickup in a camper with various other individuals. I was going to the job site by myself because my parents were working in other areas. The Border Patrol stopped our vehicle and inquired about our citizenship. I was very afraid because I did not have my birth certificate on me, I was born in Fresno. Also, the immigration raided the field next to the one I was working in and I saw how scared the individuals were who had no legal documentation to be in this

country. I vowed then that I would work for the community advocating for their rights in the legal area.

My family was very poor. We shopped at thrift stores, never threw any food away, reused any item we could, and generally struggled to survive. I learned to live very thrifty and use coupons regularly and only buy items on sale. These skills have served me well in my adult life, I always have money for a rainy day.

My family was very involved in the Catholic Church, and that saved me from getting into a lot of trouble. I still have a deep faith that guides my life every day. I was not a 4.0 student, but I tried my best in all my subjects at school. I loved school. School was fun, exciting, and interesting. It helped me to forget my life of poverty and showed me the key to my happiness and success was to continue my education. During high school, I was involved in organizations on campus that helped encourage my education. I was in the first Upward Bound Program in the Central Valley. During the summer we lived in the dorms at California State University, Fresno, and took classes in Fresno State classrooms. I loved the experience and it prepared me for my first year in college at the University of California, Berkeley.

University of California, Berkeley was a great experience for me. I took advantage of the tutoring lab and any other service to help me through my college studies. I had work-study to help pay for my education. I never lost the focus of my studies and my plan for the future to be an attorney. *Determination* and *perseverance* were my tools to keep going when everything else was falling around me. *Family, faith,* and *friends* also helped get me through the rough times.

I was accepted to the University of Michigan Law School in Ann Arbor, Michigan. The law school is one of the top twenty law schools in the United States. I decided to go there because I knew I would get a good education. I joined the organization for Latino Law Students and made many lifelong friends. I had a difficult time in law school, but I never gave up on my dream of graduating and becoming an attorney. My hardships while attending law school made me the person I am today. I love the law profession and enjoy immensely practicing law. I am bilingual and have helped many people access the legal system and understand legal procedures. It took a long time to get from the grape fields to the legal field, but I have never regretted my decision to be an attorney and look forward to a career that I can practice for the rest of my life.

Ruby Garcia is a professor of Chicano-Latino Studies. She is also a social worker. Ruby shares her life experience in the following essay, *To Dream Is to Be Successful*.

When I was a freshman in high school I knew I wanted a college education. My goal was to be a teacher or social worker. I am proud to say I accomplished both my goals. I have earned a master of social work degree (MSW) and I teach at a community college and university. My educational journey has had many obstacles. I am number seven in a family of fourteen children raised by a single parent, my mom.

My mother worked and provided for all of us. She would take us (once we were old enough) to work in the fields. We picked grapes, cotton, tomatoes, onions, figs, and at times we would work at the cutting shed cutting fresh peaches and apricots for drying. Needless to say, we grew up in poverty. Growing up poor with my thirteen siblings, I knew there was no way I could plan for a college education. I knew and felt I needed to find a job to help mom with the family income. After graduating from high school, I went to work. Before I looked for a job I went to a community college to enroll as a student. I took the entry exam, passed, and was told to come back to register for classes. I returned to register and, while waiting in line, my thoughts were of my mother and the hardships she was going through raising her children. After two hours of standing in line, a sense of duty and responsibility towards my mom and siblings overcame me. I made the decision to not enroll. Instead, I went to look for a job. It was twenty years later that I returned to community college and enrolled for classes!

I graduated from high school in 1955. During that time, there were few Mexican Americans attending college. Particularly Mexican American women! One reason was school counselors did not encourage or advise Mexican Americans to take college preparation classes. When I asked my counselor about taking college preparation classes, she said to me, "Ruby, you do not need to take these classes because you will only have babies . . ." My response was "okay." In the Mexican American culture, we were taught not to question authority.

In the Mexican American culture, women were raised and taught that we were to care for our husbands, children, and homes. That was the traditional family, but today, we have a more contemporary Mexican family. Today, the Mexican American woman has the opportunity to leave the home and pursue her goals.

In 1975, I enrolled at a community college. I was in my forties and my husband had been against my desire to attend college. But after five years of saying "O.K." to him, I finally said "No." My sons were in their teens, I was working, so I was able to afford college and pursue my educational goals. For two years I attended community college and worked. It was during this time that my work sent me to Sacramento. I worked and attended college in Sacramento for three years. In 1986, I returned to my hometown to continue my education at the university. I applied and was accepted to participate in the Bilingual Teachers Training Program (BTT). The program was for three years. The program paid for our tuition, books, and paid us a monthly stipend. I also worked for the program as a student assistant in the office headed by Dr. Robert Segura and Dr. Oscar Loya.

During my five years at the university, I took advantage of all opportunities that opened up to me. I applied and was awarded scholarships, grants, and other special programs. However, by my last two semesters I had exhausted my resources for scholarships and had to apply for financial aid and student loans. I was determined to reach my goals. In 1989, I received my bachelor of arts degree in general education with a bilingual emphasis. In 1992, I received a master of social work degree.

With the support and encouragement of my family and friends, I achieved my goals. I strongly believe that as Mexican American women, Chicanas, Latinas, however we identify ourselves, we have much potential, desire, intelligence, and motivation to follow our dreams and be successful. Whatever the obstacles may be, family, financial constraints, discrimination or prejudice. As Mexican American, Chicana, Latina women: we have and will continue to work hard for our successes.

María Solano is a bilingual school teacher. She has a master's degree and many credentials as a reading specialist. She loves teaching children to read! In the following essay, María shares her life story. The title is *First Generation Latina*.

My fondest memory as a child is sitting around the big kitchen table at four o'clock in the morning. Dad worked from sunrise to sunset. Mom was up fixing his breakfast and making his lunch. My brothers, sisters, and I would wake to the smells of *tortillas hechas a mano* and the tantalizing aroma of whatever Mom was cooking that day. We would get up, go to the restroom, and sit there with our big imploring eyes until she would have mercy and give us each a fresh burrito. We never realized the imposition we were making on her life by our demands in those early morning hours.

We were a family of thirteen, my mom, dad, six brothers and five sisters. I was one of the younger children. Based on today's standards we did not have an easy life. Dad came to this country at the age of fifteen, traveled through much of the U.S. and tried many different occupations. He had very little education, started working at a young age when his mother became a single parent to a family of five. Mom came to this country at the age of seventeen and never finished school.

My older brothers and sisters remember living in tents, sleeping on dirt floors. As the years passed and the older siblings went to work, our lives became more stable. We followed the crops for years, and then settled in Merced County. Dad was able to buy a truck for agricultural hauling. We moved to another town where he bought a ranch, then opened a camp for *braceros* coming from Mexico. This did not prove profitable for my dad because he spent too much money seeing to the comfort and well-being of the *braceros*. I still remember living in at least two different labor camps after this time. During these days we picked and processed apricots, plus we were also picking grapes for raisins.

I believe these periods of time were my epiphany! I hated working in the field and decided I would do whatever was needed to avoid this fate. I was in my teens at this time, so I started thinking that a good education could be my answer. I was already in high school, and was enrolled in college prep courses due to my elementary school grades. I went to see my high school counselor and told her I wanted to go to college. She was very gracious and told me she had wonderful beauty college scholarships to which I could apply. She was not very gracious when I told her I wanted to go to college, *college!* She stated she would not waste her time or office services because I did not have the potential to succeed in a real college. I guess it did not matter that I was an honor student. My dad and brothers thought it was a joke when I told them what had happened, they thought I was crazy, too, for considering college. My older siblings did not even have an eighth-grade diploma. I think the anger I felt at these rejections was what spurred me on to write to colleges and request assistance. I received many responses with admission forms and financial aid information. I filled them out to the best of my ability, and was granted admission to more than one college. I now possess a bachelor's degree and a master's degree. I was considering a doctorate program but then was diagnosed with cancer. I am a 9-year cancer survivor.

I married and had four children while working, going to school and raising a family. My children all have a college degree, as does my husband. My son once told me during a conversation what he wanted in life. He could do no less than get a college degree considering Dad's and my struggle to get an education. He told me that he couldn't see going backwards on the educational level. Besides, he wanted to be as smart as we were now! Needless to say, my children are still working on that, they don't have the life experiences we did, and unfortunately we may have made life too easy for our second-generation Latino children.

CHAPTER DISCUSSION QUESTIONS

1. These essays are examples of Latina literature.
   What do you feel is the main theme and/or thesis of each essay?
   Compare and contrast the main ideas presented in the essays.

2. How do you feel about the authors and the way they express themselves?
   Is their writing style effective? Is their communication effective?

3. Can you relate and identify with the authors' experiences? Please explain and give examples.

4. Do the essays help us understand Mexican American history, heritage, and culture? Explain.

5. What do you think is meant by a woman's perspective? What is your opinion in regard to the role and contribution of *Mexicanas*, Mexican American women, Chicanas, Latinas?

6. Compare and contrast the essays in terms of: 1.) creative writing, and 2.) autobiographical essay.

Xochitl

Flower

CHAPTER 10

CONCLUSION: THE STORY OF AZTLÁN AND *LA RAZA*

What, then, is the epic story of Aztlán and La Raza? Aztlán, the legendary homeland of the Azteca-Mexica, is today's homeland as declared by the Chicano Movement. La Raza is the cosmic race in Aztlán and Latino América. After hundreds of years, La Raza is the biological and cultural integration of two worlds, the Spanish European and the indigenous. Spain ties La Raza to Europe. México ties La Raza to Latino América. The United States, with its melting pot and cultural pluralism, ties La Raza to the world. Mexican American history, heritage, and culture represent a long, arduous journey. The cultural roots range from the Ice Age to the Latino world of today. This was a dynamic chronological development and evolutionary process of many years. The story of La Raza has been one of continuous social and cultural change.

Mexican Americans consider themselves an indigenous population in Aztlán. From the Chicano-Latino perspective, this is why Mexican Americans hate and despise being called *illegal aliens*. Someone may say, "Tell those damn Mexicans to go back where they came from!" So they go to *Los Angeles, Santa Barbara, San Francisco, Santa Fe, Tucsón, San Antonio*—This is where they came from! The reality is that Mexicans are here to stay! The real meaning of *indigenous* is that Mexican Americans trace their roots back to the time this land was México, and previously, Nueva España. It is no coincidence that the names of cities, counties, states, rivers, and mountain ranges are in Spanish. La Raza is Aztlán and Aztlán is La Raza. The Mexicanization of American society and culture is the past, the present, and the future.

What is the day-to-day livelihood of Latinos? Where do they work today? An intriguing and provocative look at this situation is the Hollywood production, *A Day Without a Mexican*. The movie is a satirical look at a situation where Mexicans disappear off the face of the earth and no one is there to do the everyday labor. *A Day Without a Mexican* is a comical spoof but has an underlying, thought-provoking message. For generations *Mexicanos* have interwoven themselves into the economic fabric of this country with their work ethic and exceptional labor. Today's Latinos work everywhere: agriculture, construction, factories, stores, restaurants, hotels, hospitals, schools, colleges, universities, and high-tech industries. The Latino may be the farmworker and custodian or the nurse, doctor, lawyer, scientist, engineer, movie star, or famous singer.

Latinos contribute their skill and talent in all fields and endeavors. In terms of economic power, *there are rumors that Latinos across the country spend over one million dollars per minute, 24/7!*

The mass media previously referred to Mexican Americans and Latinos as *an invisible minority*. They are now very visible on the American scene. Latinos have contributed the best of their culture and talents to this country. Surveying the landscape of American society, it appears Latinos are preserving their language and culture. From a Chicano-Latino perspective, this is the epicenter of an explosive cultural renaissance. Talent, creativity, and imagination have been unleashed. Consider the influence and impact of Latinos and their culture. Included, but not limited, is their involvement in:

Cultural arts

Hollywood (movies, directors, producers, actors and actresses)

Mass media

Music

Sports

Television

This Chicano-Latino cultural renaissance is exploding in the United States. There is a dynamic cultural interaction between the Latinos in this country and the influence from México and Latino América. The prolific Spanish-speaking media in the United States is an enormous part of the cultural equation. The culture of México and Latino América is an integral dimension of the cultural environment in the United States. In terms of the mass media, consider, for example:

Mexican and Latino music (traditional)

Mexican and Latino pop music (today's music scene)

Spanish newspapers and magazines

Spanish-speaking radio

Spanish-speaking television

The cultural span ranges from piñatas to Mexican restaurants, mariachis, and the infamous *novelas*.

Note to Students   Do a survey of the mass media produced in Spanish. Using your power of critical thinking, what is the social and cultural influence of the Spanish-speaking mass media on American society? Consider the dollars and cents question. Watch television for the Latin Grammy awards. Is this an example of the Chicano-Latino cultural renaissance?

In this new millennium, La Raza is in a unique, distinct, and at the same time, problematic situation. As a cultural group, they are the youngest and fastest-growing population in the United States. In terms of demography, *there are rumors that Latinos may be 30 percent of the U.S. population by 2050!* What is the dichotomy? On the one hand, there are countless successes in American society. Professionals abound in all fields of endeavor. Some of these professionals assimilate into the mainstream of American society and disappear into the masses. Others continue to relate and identify with their rich cultural roots. Successful Latinos and Latinas become significant positive role models for the upcoming generations. On the other hand, there are still many social issues and problems to overcome. In some neighborhoods, between a fifth and a majority of Latino youths do not graduate from high school. This is a national disaster! What are the implications for adolescents without a high school diploma? What are the implications for the country? Consider issues of poverty, gang violence, crime, addiction, domestic violence, unemployment, and just lack of life chances. It is clear that the new millennium poses challenges and opportunities. There is significant work to be done.

Latinos and Latinas can hold society accountable and responsible for not providing the opportunities necessary to succeed. At the same time, Latinos and Latinas must strive to find answers to the problems that plague the community. In the old days Chicanos used to say,

Chicano solutions to Chicano problems. This is still a viable approach. The future will see if Latinos and Latinas can forge the social and cultural change that will transform American society. The millions and millions of Latinos and Latinas will make the difference in the future of this country. The Latinoization of American society and culture is the past, the present, and the future. La Raza has lived through a prolific history and will see a prolific future.

SEMESTER DISCUSSION QUESTIONS

1. What are Mexican American Studies?
2. What is meant by Mexican American history, heritage, and culture?
3. What is meant by a Chicano and Chicana perspective?
4. What is meant by a Latino and Latina perspective?
5. What is meant by Chicano-Latino history, heritage, and culture?
6. What is meant by a Chicano-Latino analysis and perspective?
7. What are some of the main issues facing Latinos and Latinas today?
8. Identify specific social problems that face the Chicano-Latino community. Based on your research, identify specific root causes of the problems. What are specific recommendations for solving these problems?
9. What do you see as the future of Latinos and Latinas in American society?

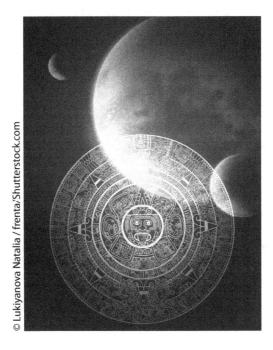

© Lukiyanova Natalia / frenta/Shutterstock.com

APPENDIX

NOTE TO STUDENTS

Critical Thinking: What is the study of demography? What are demographic characteristics?

Why is it important to understand the demographic data of a population?

How can demography assist in understanding the present condition of Latinos and future trends?

From the following census report, compile a demographic profile of the Latino population in the United States. What do you consider to be the most significant demographic characteristics?

THE HISPANIC POPULATION: 2010

2010 Census Briefs

Issued May 2011
C2010BR-04
By
Sharon R. Ennis,
Merarys Ríos-Vargas,
and
Nora G. Albert

INTRODUCTION

This report looks at an important part of our nation's changing ethnic diversity. It is part of a series that analyzes population and housing data collected from the 2010 Census, and it provides a snapshot of the Hispanic or Latino population in the United States. Hispanic population group distributions and growth at the national level and at lower levels of geography are presented.[1]

This report also provides an overview of ethnicity concepts and definitions used in the 2010 Census. The data for this report are based on the *2010 Census Summary File 1*, which is among the first 2010 Census data products to be released and is provided for each state.[2]

UNDERSTANDING HISPANIC ORIGIN DATA FROM THE 2010 CENSUS

For the 2010 Census, the question on Hispanic origin was asked of individuals living in the United States (see Figure 1). An individual's response to the Hispanic origin question was based upon self-identification. The U.S. Census Bureau collects Hispanic origin information following the guidance of the U.S. Office of Management and Budget's (OMB) 1997 *Revisions to the Standards for the Classification of Federal Data on Race and Ethnicity.*[3] These federal standards mandate that race and ethnicity (Hispanic origin) are separate and distinct concepts and that when collecting these data via self-identification, two different questions must be used.

The OMB definition of Hispanic or Latino origin used in the 2010 Census is presented in the text box "Definition of Hispanic or Latino Origin Used in the 2010 Census." OMB requires

---

[1] The terms "Hispanic or Latino" and "Hispanic" are used interchangeably in this report.

[2] The *2010 Census Summary File 1* provides data on detailed Hispanic origin groups (e.g., Mexican or Puerto Rican) and detailed information about race and tribes (e.g., Chinese, Samoan, or Choctaw). This report discusses data for the 50 states and the District of Columbia. Data for Puerto Rico are shown and discussed separately. For a detailed schedule of 2010 Census products and release dates, visit <www.census.gov/population/www/cen2010/glance/index.html>.

[3] The 1997 *Revisions to the Standards for the Classification of Federal Data on Race and Ethnicity,* issued by OMB, is available at <www.whitehouse.gov/omb/fedreg/1997standards.html>.

Figure 1.

Reproduction of the Question on Hispanic Origin From the 2010 Census

→ NOTE: Please answer BOTH Question 5 about Hispanic orgin and Question 6 about race. For this census, Hispanic orgins are not races.

5. Is this person of Hispanic, Latino, or Spanish origin?

☐ **No,** not of Hispanic, Latino, or Spanish origin?

☐ Yes, Mexican, Mexican Am., Chicano

☐ Yes, Puerto Rican

☐ Yes, Cuban

☐ Yes, another Hispanic, Latino, or Spanish origin — *print origin, for example, Argentinean, Colombian, Dominican, Nicaraguan, Salvadoran, Spaniard, and so on.*

Source: U.S. Census Bureau, 2010 Census questionnaire.

federal agencies to use a minimum of two ethnicities: Hispanic or Latino and Not Hispanic or Latino. Hispanic origin can be viewed as the heritage, nationality group, lineage, or country of birth of the person or the person's parents or ancestors before their arrival in the United States. People who identify their origin as Hispanic, Latino, or Spanish may be any race.

The question on Hispanic origin was first introduced in the 1970 Census, and subsequently a version of the question has been included in every census since.[4] Spanish surname, place of birth, and Spanish mother tongue responses were also used as identifiers of the Hispanic population in the 1970 Census and were the only Hispanic identifiers in prior censuses.[5] Over the last 40 years the question on Hispanic origin has undergone numerous changes and modifications, all with the aim of improving the quality of Hispanic origin data in the United States, Puerto Rico, and the U.S. Island Areas.[6]

The 2010 Census question on Hispanic origin included five separate response categories and one area where respondents could write in a specific Hispanic origin group. The first response category is intended for respondents who do not identify as Hispanic. The remaining response categories ("Mexican, Mexican Am., Chicano;" "Puerto Rican;" "Cuban;" and

---

[4] The Spanish origin question, now the Hispanic origin question, was originally fielded and tested by the Bureau of the Census in the November 1969 Current Population Survey. It was later used in the 1970 Census of Population (5 percent sample). The Hispanic origin question has been asked on a 100 percent basis in every census since 1980.

[5] U.S. Census Bureau, 1979, *Coverage of the Hispanic Population of the United States in the 1970 Census.* Current Population Reports, Special Studies, P-23, No. 82.

[6] The U.S. Island Areas are the U.S. Virgin Islands, American Samoa, Guam, and the Commonwealth of the Northern Mariana Islands.

"Another Hispanic, Latino, or Spanish origin") and write-in answers can be combined to create data for the OMB category of Hispanic.[7]

Definition of Hispanic or Latino Origin Used in the 2010 Census

"Hispanic or Latino" refers to a person of Cuban, Mexican, Puerto Rican, South or Central American, or other Spanish culture or origin regardless of race.

HISPANIC POPULATION

Data from the 2010 Census provide insights to our ethnically diverse nation. According to the 2010 Census, 308.7 million people resided in the United States on April 1, 2010, of which 50.5 million (or 16 percent) were of Hispanic or Latino origin (see Table 1). The Hispanic population increased from 35.3 million in 2000 when this group made up 13 percent of the total population.[8] The majority of the growth in the total population came from increases in those who reported their ethnicity as Hispanic or Latino.[9]

More than half of the growth in the total population of the United States between 2000 and 2010 was due to the increase in the Hispanic population
The Hispanic population increased by 15.2 million between 2000 and 2010, accounting for over half of the 27.3 million increase in the total population of the United States. Between 2000 and 2010, the Hispanic population grew by 43 percent, which was four times the growth in the total population at 10 percent.

Population growth between 2000 and 2010 varied by Hispanic group. The Mexican origin population increased by 54 percent and had the largest numeric change (11.2 million), growing from 20.6 million in 2000 to 31.8 million in 2010.[10] Mexicans accounted for about

---

[7] There were three changes to the Hispanic origin question for the 2010 Census. First, the wording of the question changed from "Is this person Spanish/Hispanic/Latino?" in 2000 to "Is this person of Hispanic, Latino, or Spanish origin?" in 2010. Second, in 2000, the question provided an instruction, "Mark ⊠ the **'No'** box if **not** Spanish/Hispanic/Latino." The 2010 Census question provided no specific instruction for non-Hispanic respondents. Third, in 2010, the "Yes, another Hispanic, a Latino, or Spanish origin" category provided examples of six Hispanic origin groups (Argentinean, Colombian, Dominican, Nicaraguan, Salvadoran, Spaniard, and so on) and instructed respondents to "print origin." In 2000, no Hispanic origin examples were given.

[8] The observed changes in Hispanic origin counts between Census 2000 and the 2010 Census could be attributed to a number of factors. Demographic change since 2000, which includes births and deaths in a geographic area and migration in and out of a geographic area, will have an impact on the resulting 2010 Census counts. Some changes in the Hispanic origin question's wording and format since Census 2000 could have influenced reporting patterns in the 2010 Census. Additionally, changes to the Hispanic origin edit and coding procedures could have impacted the 2010 counts. These factors should especially be considered when observing changes for detailed Hispanic groups.

[9] For the purposes of this report, the term "reported" is used to refer to the response provided by respondents as well as responses assigned during the editing and imputation process.

Table 1.
Hispanic or Latino Origin Population by Type: 2000 and 2010

(For information on confidentiality protection, nonsampling error, and definitions, see *www.census.gov/prod/cen2010/doc/sf1.pdf*)

Origin and type	2000		2010		Change, 2000 to 2010[1]	
	Number	Percent of total	Number	Percent of total	Number	Percent
HISPANIC OR LATINO ORIGIN						
Total	**281,421,906**	100.0	**308,745,538**	100.0	**27,323,632**	**9.7**
Hispanic or Latino	35,305,818	12.5	50,477,594	16.3	15,171,776	43.0
Not Hispanic or Latino..........................	246,116,088	87.5	258,267,944	83.7	12,151,856	4.9
HISPANIC OR LATINO BY TYPE						
Total	**35,305,818**	100.0	**50,477,594**	100.0	**15,171,776**	**43.0**
Mexican......................................	20,640,711	58.5	31,798,258	63.0	11,157,547	54.1
Puerto Rican	3,406,178	9.6	4,623,716	9.2	1,217,538	35.7
Cuban	1,241,685	3.5	1,785,547	3.5	543,862	43.8
Other Hispanic or Latino	10,017,244	28.4	12,270,073	24.3	2,252,829	22.5
Dominican (Dominican Republic)................	764,945	2.2	1,414,703	2.8	649,758	84.9
Central American (excludes Mexican)	1,686,937	4.8	3,998,280	7.9	2,311,343	137.0
Costa Rican	68,588	0.2	126,418	0.3	57,830	84.3
Guatemalan	372,487	1.1	1,044,209	2.1	671,722	180.3
Honduran	217,569	0.6	633,401	1.3	415,832	191.1
Nicaraguan..............................	177,684	0.5	348,202	0.7	170,518	96.0
Panamanian.............................	91,723	0.3	165,456	0.3	73,733	80.4
Salvadoran..............................	655,165	1.9	1,648,968	3.3	993,803	151.7
Other Central American[2]	103,721	0.3	31,626	0.1	−72,095	−69.5
South American.............................	1,353,562	3.8	2,769,434	5.5	1,415,872	104.6
Argentinean	100,864	0.3	224,952	0.4	124,088	123.0
Bolivian.................................	42,068	0.1	99,210	0.2	57,142	135.8
Chilean.................................	68,849	0.2	126,810	0.3	57,961	84.2
Colombian	470,684	1.3	908,734	1.8	438,050	93.1
Ecuadorian..............................	260,559	0.7	564,631	1.1	304,072	116.7
Paraguayan	8,769	–	20,023	–	11,254	128.3
Peruvian................................	233,926	0.7	531,358	1.1	297,432	127.1
Uruguayan	18,804	0.1	56,884	0.1	38,080	202.5
Venezuelan..............................	91,507	0.3	215,023	0.4	123,516	135.0
Other South American[3].....................	57,532	0.2	21,809	–	−35,723	−62.1
Spaniard...................................	100,135	0.3	635,253	1.3	535,118	534.4
All other Hispanic or Latino[4].....................	6,111,665	17.3	3,452,403	6.8	−2,659,262	−43.5

– Percentage rounds to 0.0.

[1] The observed changes in Hispanic origin counts between Census 2000 and the 2010 Census could be attributed to a number of factors. Demographic change since 2000, which includes births and deaths in a geographic area and migration in and out of a geographic area, will have an impact on the resulting 2010 Census counts. Some changes in the Hispanic origin question's wording and format since Census 2000 could have influenced reporting patterns in the 2010 Census. Additionally, changes to the Hispanic origin edit and coding procedures could have impacted the 2010 counts. These factors should especially be considered when observing changes for detailed Hispanic groups.

[2] This category includes people who reported Central American Indian groups, "Canal Zone," and "Central American."

[3] This category includes people who reported South American Indian groups and "South American."

[4] This category includes people who reported "Hispanic" or "Latino" and other general terms.

Sources: U.S. Census Bureau, *Census 2000 Summary File 1* and *2010 Census Summary File 1.*

[10] "People of Mexican origin" refers to people who report their origin as Mexican. It can include people born in Mexico, in the United States, or in other countries. This holds true for all the detailed Hispanic origin groups discussed in this report (e.g., people of Cuban origin, Salvadoran origin, etc). The question on Hispanic origin is an ethnicity question and not a place of birth question. All Hispanic origin responses are based on self-identification. Throughout this report, terms such as Mexican origin and Mexicans or Cuban origin and Cubans are used interchangeably, and in all cases refer to the ethnic origin of the person, not exclusively their place of birth or nationality.

three-quarters of the 15.2 million increase in the Hispanic population from 2000 to 2010. Puerto Ricans grew by 36 percent, increasing from 3.4 million to 4.6 million. The Cuban population increased by 44 percent, growing from 1.2 million in 2000 to 1.8 million in 2010. Hispanics who reported other origins increased by 22 percent, from 10.0 million to 12.3 million.

Other Hispanic Origins Refer to A Variety of Identifications

Among the 12.3 million Hispanics who were classified as Other Hispanic in 2010, 1.4 million were of Dominican origin, 4.0 million were of Central American origin (other than Mexican), 2.8 million were of South American origin, 635,000 were Spaniard, and 3.5 million reported general terms such as "Hispanic" or "Latino."

Among Central American Hispanics (excluding Mexicans), those of Salvadoran origin were the largest group at 1.6 million, followed by Guatemalans (1.0 million) and Hondurans (633,000). Of the South American Hispanic population, those of Colombian origin were the largest group at 909,000, followed by Ecuadorians at 565,000 and Peruvians at 531,000.

Although people of Mexican, Puerto Rican, and Cuban origin were the largest detailed Hispanic groups, they grew at slower rates than the other detailed groups. Over the decade, the Spaniard population showed the largest percent increase. The Spaniard population in 2010 was more than six times larger than reported in 2000, increasing from 100,000 to 635,000. Other Hispanic groups with origins from Central and South America (Uruguayan, Honduran, Guatemalan, Salvadoran, Bolivian, Venezuelan, Paraguayan, Peruvian, Argentinean, and Ecuadorian) also showed large percent increases, increasing to more than twice their population sizes from 2000 to 2010.

All detailed Hispanic groups showed large percentage increases between 2000 and 2010. On the other hand, the "Other Central American," "Other South American," and "All other Hispanic or Latino" groups—which include general terms such as Central American, South American, and Latino—experienced large percentage decreases during this period.[11,12] The "Other Central American" group declined from about 104,000 in 2000 to 32,000 in 2010, decreasing 70 percent. The "Other South American" group decreased from about 58,000 to 22,000 (down 62 percent). The "All other Hispanic or Latino" group decreased by 44 percent, from 6.1 million in 2000 to 3.5 million in 2010.

---

[11] "Other Central American" includes people who reported Central American Indian groups, "Canal Zone," and "Central American." "Other South American" includes people who reported South American Indian groups and "South American." "Other Hispanic or Latino" includes people who reported "Hispanic" or "Latino" and other general terms.

[12] Empirical evidence of question-design effects on the question of Hispanic origin is well documented in several Census Bureau studies. Results for the Census 2000 Alternative Questionnaire Experiment for example, showed changes in wording and omission of specific Hispanic origin examples contributed to a significant number of people reporting general Hispanic terms such as "Hispanic" and "Latino" instead of reporting a specific Hispanic origin group such as Colombian or Dominican. For more information, see *Questionnaire Effects on Reporting of Race and Hispanic Origin: Results of a Replication of the 1990 Mail Short Form in Census 2000* at <www.census.gov/pred/www/rpts/AQE%20R&HO%20Final%20Report.pdf> and *Results of the 2003 National Census Test of Race and Hispanic Questions* at <www.census.gov/srd/papers/pdf/rsm2007-34.pdf>.

About three-quarters of Hispanics reported as Mexican, Puerto Rican, or Cuban origin

In 2010, people of Mexican origin comprised the largest Hispanic group, representing 63 percent of the total Hispanic population in the United States (up from 58 percent in 2000) as shown in Figure 2. The second largest group was Puerto Rican, which comprised 9 percent of the Hispanic population in 2010 (down from 10 percent in 2000). The Cuban population represented approximately 4 percent of the total Hispanic population in both the 2000 and 2010 censuses. These three groups accounted for about three-quarters of the Hispanic population in the United States.

Figure 2.
PERCENT DISTRIBUTION OF THE HISPANIC POPULATION BY TYPE OF ORIGIN: 2010

(For more information on confidentiality protection, nonsampling error, and definitions, see *www.census.gov/prod/cen2010/doc/sf1.pdf*)

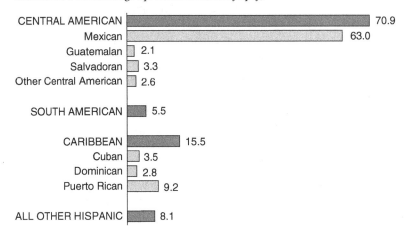

Notes:

1) The "Other Central American" group includes people who reported "Costa Rican," "Honduran," "Nicaraguan," "Panamanian," Central American Indian groups, "Canal Zone," and "Central American."

2) The "South American" group includes people who reported "Argentinean," "Bolivian," "Chilean," "Colombian," "Ecuadorian," "Paraguayan," "Peruvian," "Uruguayan," "Venezuelan," South American Indian groups, and "South American."

3) The "All Other Hispanic" group includes people who reported "Spaniard," as well as "Hispanic" or "Latino" and other general terms.

Source: U.S. Census Bureau, *2010 Census Summary File 1.*

Central American Hispanics, including Mexicans, represented 71 percent of the total Hispanic population residing in the United States. There were 1.6 million people of Salvadoran origin (3 percent of the total Hispanic population) in 2010, rising from 655,000 in 2000. The Salvadoran population grew significantly between 2000 and 2010, increasing by 152 percent. Between 2000 and 2010, Guatemalans increased considerably, growing by 180 percent. Guatemalans represented 2 percent of the total Hispanic population in 2010. This population rose from 372,000 in 2000 to over 1 million in 2010.

South American Hispanics grew by 105 percent, increasing from 1.4 million in 2000 to 2.8 million in 2010. The South American Hispanic population represented 5 percent of the total Hispanic population in 2010.

Dominicans accounted for 3 percent of the total Hispanic population in the United States. This population grew by 85 percent, increasing from 765,000 in 2000 to 1.4 million in 2010. The remaining Hispanic origin groups represented about 8 percent of the total Hispanic population in the United States (see Figure 2).

GEOGRAPHIC DISTRIBUTION

More Than Three-Quarters of the Hispanic Population Lived in the West or South[13]

In 2010, 41 percent of Hispanics lived in the West and 36 percent lived in the South. The Northeast and Midwest accounted for 14 percent and 9 percent, respectively, of the Hispanic population.

Hispanics accounted for 29 percent of the population in the West, the only region in which Hispanics exceeded the national level of 16 percent (see Table 2). Hispanics accounted for 16 percent of the population of the South, 13 percent of the Northeast, and 7 percent of the Midwest's population.

The Hispanic population grew in every region between 2000 and 2010, and most significantly in the South and Midwest. The South experienced a growth of 57 percent in its Hispanic population, which was four times the growth of the total population in the South (14 percent). Significant growth also occurred in the Midwest, with the Hispanic population increasing by 49 percent. This was more than twelve times the growth of the total population in the Midwest (4 percent).

---

[13] The Northeast census region includes Connecticut, Maine, Massachusetts, New Hampshire, New Jersey, New York, Pennsylvania, Rhode Island, and Vermont. The Midwest census region includes Illinois, Indiana, Iowa, Kansas, Michigan, Minnesota, Missouri, Nebraska, North Dakota, Ohio, South Dakota, and Wisconsin. The South census region includes Alabama, Arkansas, Delaware, the District of Columbia, Florida, Georgia, Kentucky, Louisiana, Maryland, Mississippi, North Carolina, Oklahoma, South Carolina, Tennessee, Texas, Virginia, and West Virginia. The West census region includes Alaska, Arizona, California, Colorado, Hawaii, Idaho, Montana, Nevada, New Mexico, Oregon, Utah, Washington, and Wyoming.

Table 2.
Hispanic or Latino Population for the United States, Regions, and States, and for Puerto Rico: 2000 and 2010
(For information on confidentiality protection, nonsampling error, and definitions, see *www.census.gov/prod/cen2010/doc/sf1.pdf*)

Area	2000			2010			Population change, 2000 to 2010			
		Hispanic or Latino			Hispanic or Latino		Total		Hispanic or Latino	
	Total	Number	Percent of total population	Total	Number	Percent of total population	Number	Per- cent	Number	Per- cent
United States...	281,421,906	35,305,818	12.5	308,745,538	50,477,594	16.3	27,323,632	9.7	15,171,776	43.0
REGION										
Northeast..........	53,594,378	5,254,087	9.8	55,317,240	6,991,969	12.6	1,722,862	3.2	1,737,882	33.1
Midwest............	64,392,776	3,124,532	4.9	66,927,001	4,661,678	7.0	2,534,225	3.9	1,537,146	49.2
South..............	100,236,820	11,586,696	11.6	114,555,744	18,227,508	15.9	14,318,924	14.3	6,640,812	57.3
West	63,197,932	15,340,503	24.3	71,945,553	20,596,439	28.6	8,747,621	13.8	5,255,936	34.3
STATE										
Alabama	4,447,100	75,830	1.7	4,779,736	185,602	3.9	332,636	7.5	109,772	144.8
Alaska	626,932	25,852	4.1	710,231	39,249	5.5	83,299	13.3	13,397	51.8
Arizona	5,130,632	1,295,617	25.3	6,392,017	1,895,149	29.6	1,261,385	24.6	599,532	46.3
Arkansas	2,673,400	86,866	3.2	2,915,918	186,050	6.4	242,518	9.1	99,184	114.2
California	33,871,648	10,966,556	32.4	37,253,956	14,013,719	37.6	3,382,308	10.0	3,047,163	27.8
Colorado	4,301,261	735,601	17.1	5,029,196	1,038,687	20.7	727,935	16.9	303,086	41.2
Connecticut	3,405,565	320,323	9.4	3,574,097	479,087	13.4	168,532	4.9	158,764	49.6
Delaware	783,600	37,277	4.8	897,934	73,221	8.2	114,334	14.6	35,944	96.4
District of Columbia	572,059	44,953	7.9	601,723	54,749	9.1	29,664	5.2	9,796	21.8
Florida	15,982,378	2,682,715	16.8	18,801,310	4,223,806	22.5	2,818,932	17.6	1,541,091	57.4
Georgia	8,186,453	435,227	5.3	9,687,653	853,689	8.8	1,501,200	18.3	418,462	96.1
Hawaii	1,211,537	87,699	7.2	1,360,301	120,842	8.9	148,764	12.3	33,143	37.8
Idaho	1,293,953	101,690	7.9	1,567,582	175,901	11.2	273,629	21.1	74,211	73.0
Illinois............	12,419,293	1,530,262	12.3	12,830,632	2,027,578	15.8	411,339	3.3	497,316	32.5
Indiana............	6,080,485	214,536	3.5	6,483,802	389,707	6.0	403,317	6.6	175,171	81.7
Iowa..............	2,926,324	82,473	2.8	3,046,355	151,544	5.0	120,031	4.1	69,071	83.7
Kansas............	2,688,418	188,252	7.0	2,853,118	300,042	10.5	164,700	6.1	111,790	59.4
Kentucky	4,041,769	59,939	1.5	4,339,367	132,836	3.1	297,598	7.4	72,897	121.6
Louisiana	4,468,976	107,738	2.4	4,533,372	192,560	4.2	64,396	1.4	84,822	78.7
Maine.............	1,274,923	9,360	0.7	1,328,361	16,935	1.3	53,438	4.2	7,575	80.9
Maryland	5,296,486	227,916	4.3	5,773,552	470,632	8.2	477,066	9.0	242,716	106.5
Massachusetts........	6,349,097	428,729	6.8	6,547,629	627,654	9.6	198,532	3.1	198,925	46.4
Michigan	9,938,444	323,877	3.3	9,883,640	436,358	4.4	−54,804	−0.6	112,481	34.7
Minnesota	4,919,479	143,382	2.9	5,303,925	250,258	4.7	384,446	7.8	106,876	74.5
Mississippi.........	2,844,658	39,569	1.4	2,967,297	81,481	2.7	122,639	4.3	41,912	105.9
Missouri...........	5,595,211	118,592	2.1	5,988,927	212,470	3.5	393,716	7.0	93,878	79.2
Montana...........	902,195	18,081	2.0	989,415	28,565	2.9	87,220	9.7	10,484	58.0
Nebraska..........	1,711,263	94,425	5.5	1,826,341	167,405	9.2	115,078	6.7	72,980	77.3
Nevada	1,998,257	393,970	19.7	2,700,551	716,501	26.5	702,294	35.1	322,531	81.9
New Hampshire.......	1,235,786	20,489	1.7	1,316,470	36,704	2.8	80,684	6.5	16,215	79.1
New Jersey	8,414,350	1,117,191	13.3	8,791,894	1,555,144	17.7	377,544	4.5	437,953	39.2
New Mexico.........	1,819,046	765,386	42.1	2,059,179	953,403	46.3	240,133	13.2	188,017	24.6
New York	18,976,457	2,867,583	15.1	19,378,102	3,416,922	17.6	401,645	2.1	549,339	19.2
North Carolina........	8,049,313	378,963	4.7	9,535,483	800,120	8.4	1,486,170	18.5	421,157	111.1
North Dakota	642,200	7,786	1.2	672,591	13,467	2.0	30,391	4.7	5,681	73.0
Ohio..............	11,353,140	217,123	1.9	11,536,504	354,674	3.1	183,364	1.6	137,551	63.4
Oklahoma	3,450,654	179,304	5.2	3,751,351	332,007	8.9	300,697	8.7	152,703	85.2
Oregon............	3,421,399	275,314	8.0	3,831,074	450,062	11.7	409,675	12.0	174,748	63.5
Pennsylvania	12,281,054	394,088	3.2	12,702,379	719,660	5.7	421,325	3.4	325,572	82.6
Rhode Island........	1,048,319	90,820	8.7	1,052,567	130,655	12.4	4,248	0.4	39,835	43.9
South Carolina.......	4,012,012	95,076	2.4	4,625,364	235,682	5.1	613,352	15.3	140,606	147.9
South Dakota........	754,844	10,903	1.4	814,180	22,119	2.7	59,336	7.9	11,216	102.9
Tennessee..........	5,689,283	123,838	2.2	6,346,105	290,059	4.6	656,822	11.5	166,221	134.2
Texas.............	20,851,820	6,669,666	32.0	25,145,561	9,460,921	37.6	4,293,741	20.6	2,791,255	41.8
Utah..............	2,233,169	201,559	9.0	2,763,885	358,340	13.0	530,716	23.8	156,781	77.8
Vermont...........	608,827	5,504	0.9	625,741	9,208	1.5	16,914	2.8	3,704	67.3
Virginia............	7,078,515	329,540	4.7	8,001,024	631,825	7.9	922,509	13.0	302,285	91.7
Washington	5,894,121	441,509	7.5	6,724,540	755,790	11.2	830,419	14.1	314,281	71.2
West Virginia	1,808,344	12,279	0.7	1,852,994	22,268	1.2	44,650	2.5	9,989	81.4
Wisconsin	5,363,675	192,921	3.6	5,686,986	336,056	5.9	323,311	6.0	143,135	74.2
Wyoming	493,782	31,669	6.4	563,626	50,231	8.9	69,844	14.1	18,562	58.6
Puerto Rico	3,808,610	3,762,746	98.8	3,725,789	3,688,455	99.0	−82,821	−2.2	−74,291	−2.0

Sources: U.S. Census Bureau, *Census 2000 Summary File 1* and *2010 Census Summary File 1.*

While the Hispanic population grew at a slower rate in the West and Northeast, significant growth still occurred between 2000 and 2010. The Hispanic population grew by 34 percent in the West, which was more than twice the growth of the total population in the West (14 percent). The Northeast's Hispanic population grew by 33 percent—ten times the growth in the total population of the Northeast (3 percent).

Among Hispanic groups with a population of one million or more in 2010, three of the largest Central American groups were concentrated in the West. About two-fifths of people with origins from Guatemala and EI Salvador (38 percent and 40 percent, respectively) and half with Mexican origin (52 percent) resided in the West (see Table 3). Unlike Guatemalans, Mexicans, and Salvadorans, all Other Central Americans were more likely to reside in the South.[14] More than half of all Other Central Americans (53 percent) lived in the South, while 21.9 percent lived in the West. Mexicans were less likely to reside in the Northeast (3 percent) than Guatemalans, Salvadorans, and Other Central Americans.

South American Hispanics were less likely to reside in the West and more likely to reside in the Northeast than the Central American Hispanic groups. About two-fifths of South American Hispanics (42 percent) lived in the South, 37 percent in the Northeast, 15 percent in the West, and 6 percent in the Midwest.

The largest Caribbean Hispanic groups were concentrated in different regions of the United States. Compared to Central and South American Hispanics, the Cuban, Dominican, and Puerto Rican origin populations were less likely to reside in the West. Cubans were much more likely to live in the South and Dominicans and Puerto Ricans were more likely to live in the Northeast. More than three-quarters of the Cuban population (77 percent) resided in the South, more than three-quarters of Dominicans (78 percent) resided in the Northeast, and more than half of the Puerto Rican population (53 percent) lived in the Northeast.

Over half of the Hispanic population in the United States resided in just three states: California, Texas, and Florida

In 2010, 37.6 million, or 75 percent, of Hispanics lived in the eight states with Hispanic populations of one million or more (California, Texas, Florida, New York, Illinois, Arizona, New Jersey, and Colorado). Hispanics in California accounted for 14.0 million (28 percent) of the total Hispanic population, while the Hispanic population in Texas accounted for 9.5 million (19 percent) as shown in Figure 3. Hispanics in Florida accounted for 4.2 million (8 percent) of the U.S. Hispanic population.

---

[14] The "Other Central American" group shown in Table 3 is different than the group with the same name shown in Table 1. The "Other Central American" group in Table 1 includes people who reported Central American Indian groups, "Canal Zone," and "Central American." The "Other Central American" group in Table 3 includes people who reported "Costa Rican," "Honduran," "Nicaraguan," "Panamanian," Central American Indian groups, "Canal Zone," and "Central American."

Table 3.

Detailed Hispanic or Latino Origin Groups With a Population Size of One Million or More for the United States and Regions: 2010

(For information on confidentiality protection, nonsampling error, and definitions, see *www.census.gov/prod/cen2010/doc/sf1.pdf*)

Origin	United States		Northeast		Midwest		South		West	
	Number	Percent	Number	Percent	Number	Percent	Number	Percent	Number	Percent
Total Hispanic	50,477,594	100.0	6,991,969	13.9	4,661,678	9.2	18,227,508	36.1	20,596,439	40.8
Central American.	35,796,538	100.0	1,644,749	4.6	3,700,814	10.3	12,642,799	35.3	17,808,176	49.7
Mexican	31,798,258	100.0	918,188	2.9	3,470,726	10.9	10,945,244	34.4	16,464,100	51.8
Guatemalan	1,044,209	100.0	203,931	19.5	95,588	9.2	348,287	33.4	396,403	38.0
Salvadoran.	1,648,968	100.0	270,509	16.4	61,894	3.8	655,184	39.7	661,381	40.1
Other Central American[1] . .	1,305,103	100.0	252,121	19.3	72,606	5.6	694,084	53.2	286,292	21.9
South American[2]	2,769,434	100.0	1,033,473	37.3	158,768	5.7	1,150,536	41.5	426,657	15.4
Caribbean	7,823,966	100.0	3,745,150	47.9	523,524	6.7	3,008,377	38.5	546,915	7.0
Cuban	1,785,547	100.0	197,173	11.0	62,990	3.5	1,376,453	77.1	148,931	8.3
Dominican	1,414,703	100.0	1,104,802	78.1	25,799	1.8	258,383	18.3	25,719	1.8
Puerto Rican	4,623,716	100.0	2,443,175	52.8	434,735	9.4	1,373,541	29.7	372,265	8.1
All other Hispanic[3]	4,087,656	100.0	568,597	13.9	278,572	6.8	1,425,796	34.9	1,814,691	44.4

[1] This category includes people who reported "Costa Rican," "Honduran," "Nicaraguan," "Panamanian," Central American Indian groups, "Canal Zone," and "Central American."

[2] This category includes people who reported "Argentinean," "Bolivian," "Chilean," "Colombian," "Ecuadorian," "Paraguayan," "Peruvian," "Uruguayan," "Venezuelan," South American Indian groups, and "South American."

[3] This category includes people who reported "Spaniard," as well as "Hispanic" or "Latino" and other general terms.

Source: U.S. Census Bureau, 2010 Census special tabulation.

The Hispanic population experienced growth between 2000 and 2010 in all 50 states and the District of Columbia. The Hispanic population in eight states in the South (Alabama, Arkansas, Kentucky, Maryland, Mississippi, North Carolina, South Carolina, and Tennessee) and South Dakota more than doubled in size between 2000 and 2010. However, even with this large growth, the percent Hispanic in 2010 for each of these states remained less than 9 percent, far below the national level of 16 percent. The Hispanic population in South Carolina grew the fastest, increasing from 95,000 in 2000 to 236,000 in 2010 (a 148 percent increase). Alabama showed the second fastest rate of growth at 145 percent, increasing from 76,000 to 186,000.

Hispanics in New Mexico were 46 percent of the total state population, the highest proportion for any state. Hispanics were 16 percent (the national level) or more of the state population in eight other states (Arizona, California, Colorado, Florida, Nevada, New Jersey, New York, and Texas). Hispanics accounted for less than 16 percent of the population in 41 states and the District of Columbia.

The top five states for detailed Hispanic origin groups with a national population size of one million or more in 2010 are shown in Table 4. More than one-half (61 percent) of the Mexican origin population in the United States resided in California (11.4 million) and Texas (8.0 million) alone. About two-fifths (41 percent) of the Puerto Rican population lived in two

Figure 3.

Percent Distribution of the Hispanic Population by State: 2010

(For more information on confidentiality protection, nonsampling error, and definitions, see *www.census.gov/prod/cen2010/doc/sf1.pdf*)

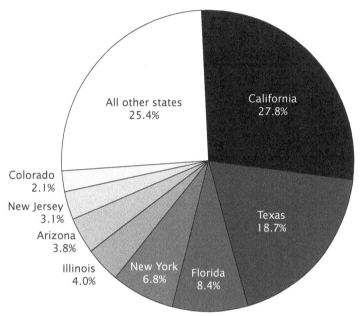

Source: U.S. Census Bureau, *2010 Census Summary File 1.*

states, New York (1.1 million) and Florida (848,000). More than two-thirds (68 percent) of all Cubans lived in one state: Florida (1.2 million). Dominicans were highly concentrated in the state of New York with nearly half of them residing there in 2010 (675,000 or 48 percent). About one-third (32 percent) of people of Guatemalan origin resided in California (333,000) and nearly half (48 percent) of the Salvadoran population was concentrated in California (574,000) and Texas (223,000). The remaining other Hispanic origin groups with less than one million in population size were concentrated in California (1.4 million or 17 percent), Florida (1.2 million or 15 percent), Texas (1.0 million or 13 percent), New York (918,000 or 11 percent), and New Jersey (517,000 or 6 percent).

Table 4.

Top Five States for Detailed Hispanic or Latino Origin Groups With a Population Size of One Million or More in the United States: 2010

(For information on confidentiality protection, nonsampling error, and definitions, see *www.census.gov/prod/cen2010/doc/sf1.pdf*)

Origin	Total	Rank				
		First	Second	Third	Fourth	Fifth
MEXICAN						
Area................	United States	California	Texas	Arizona	Illinois	Colorado
Population	31,798,258	11,423,146	7,951,193	1,657,668	1,602,403	757,181
PUERTO RICAN						
Area................	United States	New York	Florida	New Jersey	Pennsylvania	Massachusetts
Population	4,623,716	1,070,558	847,550	434,092	366,082	266,125
CUBAN						
Area................	United States	Florida	California	New Jersey	New York	Texas
Population	1,785,547	1,213,438	88,607	83,362	70,803	46,541
DOMINICAN						
Area................	United States	New York	New Jersey	Florida	Massachusetts	Pennsylvania
Population	1,414,703	674,787	197,922	172,451	103,292	62,348
GUATEMALAN						
Area................	United States	California	Florida	New York	Texas	New Jersey
Population	1,044,209	332,737	83,882	73,806	66,244	48,869
SALVADORAN						
Area................	United States	California	Texas	New York	Virginia	Maryland
Population	1,648,968	573,956	222,599	152,130	123,800	123,789
OTHER HISPANIC[1]						
Area................	United States	California	Florida	Texas	New York	New Jersey
Population	8,162,193	1,393,873	1,221,623	1,030,415	917,550	516,652

[1] This category includes all remaining Hispanic groups with population size less than 1 million.

Source: U.S. Census Bureau, *2010 Census Summary File 1.*

Salvadorans were the largest Hispanic group in the nation's capital

The Mexican origin population represented the largest Hispanic group in 40 states, with more than half of these states in the South and West regions of the country, two in the Northeast region, and in all 12 states in the Midwest region (see Figure 4). Meanwhile Puerto Ricans were the largest group in six of the nine states in the Northeast region and in one Western state, Hawaii (44,000). Dominicans were the largest group in one Northeastern state, Rhode Island (35,000). In the South region, Cubans were the largest Hispanic origin group in Florida (1.2 million) and Salvadorans were the largest group in Maryland (124,000) and the District of Columbia (17,000).

The Commonwealth of Puerto Rico was 99 percent Hispanic

Although the vast majority of the total population in Puerto Rico was of Hispanic origin (99 percent), the total population declined since Census 2000, from 3.8 million to 3.7 million in 2010. Puerto Ricans made up 96 percent of all Hispanics on the island and accounted for 83 percent of the total population loss. On the other hand, the Dominican population, the

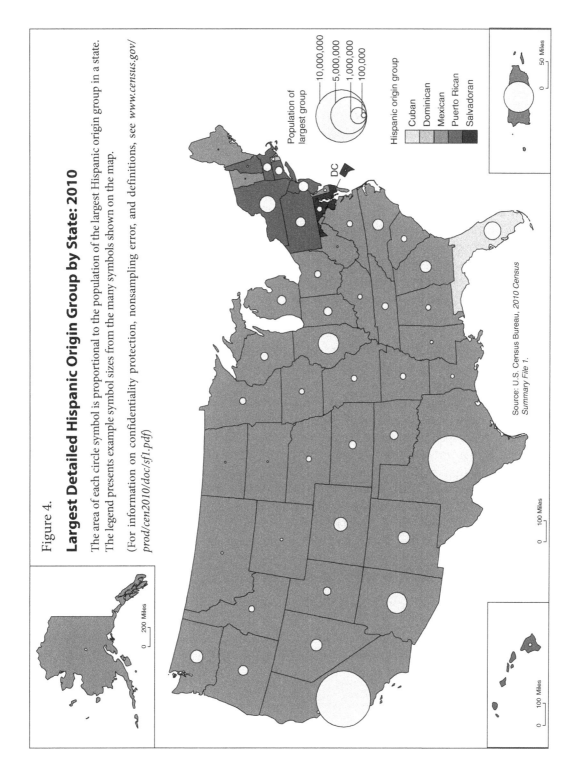

Figure 4.

Largest Detailed Hispanic Origin Group by State: 2010

The area of each circle symbol is proportional to the population of the largest Hispanic origin group in a state. The legend presents example symbol sizes from the many symbols shown on the map.

(For information on confidentiality protection, nonsampling error, and definitions, see *www.census.gov/ prod/cen2010/doc/sf1.pdf)*

Population of largest group

10,000,000
5,000,000
1,000,000
100,000

Hispanic origin group

Cuban
Dominican
Mexican
Puerto Rican
Salvadoran

DC

Source: U.S. Census Bureau, *2010 Census Summary File 1.*

0   200 Miles

0   100 Miles

0   100 Miles

0   50 Miles

second largest Hispanic group on the island, increased by 21 percent or 12,000 since Census 2010.[15] Dominicans made up 2 percent of all Hispanics on the island.

Counties with the highest proportions of Hispanics were along the southwestern border of the United States

Hispanics were concentrated in bands of counties along the states bordering Mexico (Texas, New Mexico, Arizona, and California). They were also concentrated outside these four states. In particular, Hispanic concentrations occurred in counties within central Washington, in counties within the states of Kansas, Idaho, Oklahoma, Nebraska, and Colorado, in counties around Chicago, and along the East Coast from New York to Virginia, in counties within central and southern Florida, and the District of Columbia (see Figure 5).

Hispanics were the majority of the population in 82 out of 3,143 counties, accounting for 16 percent of the total Hispanic population.[16] In the South, Hispanics were the majority in 51 counties in Texas and one (Miami-Dade) in Florida. In the West, Hispanics were the majority in 12 counties in New Mexico, nine counties in California and two counties in each of the following states: Arizona (Santa Cruz and Yuma), Colorado (Conejos and Costilla), and Washington (Adams and Franklin). In the Midwest, Hispanics were the majority in two counties in Kansas (Ford and Seward), and in the Northeast, Hispanics were the majority in one county (Bronx) in New York.

In 2010, the proportion of Hispanics within a county exceeded the national level (16 percent) most often in the counties of the South and West, especially in counties along the border with Mexico. Hispanics exceeded the national level of 16 percent of the total population in 429 counties, 14 percent of all counties. Hispanics represented one-quarter to less than half of the county population in 177 counties. The percent Hispanic exceeded the national level of 16 percent but was less than 25.0 percent of the population in 170 counties. More than 86 percent of all counties (2,714 counties) were below the national level. The percent Hispanic ranged from 5.0 percent to just under the national level in 721 counties and were less than 5.0 percent of the county's population in the majority of the U.S. counties (1,993 of the nation's 3,143 counties).

More than 4 million Hispanics lived in Los Angeles County, California

In 2010, Hispanics in eight counties (all counties with one million or more Hispanics) accounted for one-fourth (27 percent) of the total Hispanic population. There were 4.7 million Hispanics in Los Angeles County, California; 1.7 million in Harris County, Texas; 1.6 million in Miami-Dade County, Florida; 1.2 million in Cook County, Illinois; 1.1 million

---

[15] For more information, see the 2010 *Census Summary File 1*.

[16] The counties where Hispanics were the majority of the total population are represented by the More than 50.0 percent class in Figure 5.

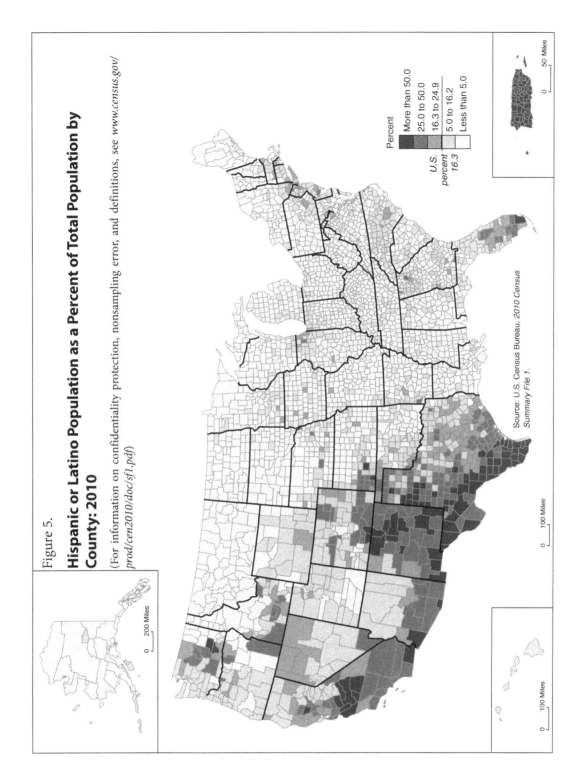

Figure 5.

Hispanic or Latino Population as a Percent of Total Population by County: 2010

(For information on confidentiality protection, nonsampling error, and definitions, see *www.census.gov/ prod/cen2010/doc/sf1.pdf*)

Percent

More than 50.0

25.0 to 50.0

16.3 to 24.9

5.0 to 16.2

Less than 5.0

U.S. percent 16.3

Source: U.S. Census Bureau, *2010 Census Summary File 1.*

0   50 Miles

0   100 Miles

0   100 Miles

0   200 Miles

in Maricopa County, Arizona; and 1.0 million in each of the following counties: Orange, California; Bexar, Texas; and San Bernardino, California.

Hispanics increased to more than twice their size since 2000 in at least 1 in every 4 counties.

Of the 3,143 counties in the United States, Hispanics doubled or more in population size in 912 counties (see Figure 6). Among the counties with at least 10,000 or more Hispanics in 2010 (469 counties), the top five fastest growing counties were Luzerne, Pennsylvania (479 percent change); Henry, Georgia (339 percent change); Kendall, Illinois (338 percent change); Douglas, Georgia (321 percent change); and Shelby, Alabama (297 percent change).

More than two-thirds of all counties (69 percent) had a percent change since Census 2000 higher than the national average, 43 percent. About 6 percent of all these counties were in the state of Georgia (129 counties).

On the other hand, only 6 percent of all counties (178 counties) showed a negative percent change for the Hispanic population. More than 90 percent of these counties (165 counties) had less than five thousand Hispanics in 2010.

In 2010, more than four million Hispanics lived in the cities of New York and Los Angeles[17]

Between 500,000 and 1,000,000 Hispanics resided in Houston, San Antonio, Chicago, Phoenix, El Paso, and Dallas (see Table 5). San Diego and San Jose, California, had between 300,000 and 500,000 Hispanics.

In what places were Hispanics the majority?

Hispanics in East Los Angeles, California, were 97 percent (123,000) of the total population, the highest for any place outside the Commonwealth of Puerto Rico with 100,000 or more total population (see Table 5). Hispanics were the majority of the population in 27 other places with at least 100,000 total population in 2010.[18] Two of the top ten places in terms of numbers of Hispanics, El Paso, Texas, and San Antonio, Texas, also had a majority who were Hispanic (81 percent and 63 percent, respectively).

---

[17] About two in three (68 percent) Hispanics in the state of New York resided in the five boroughs that make up New York City: 741,000 in the Bronx, 614,000 in Queens, 496,000 in Brooklyn, 404,000 in Manhattan, and 81,000 in Staten Island.

[18] Hispanics were the majority of the population in the ten places shown in Table 5 as well as in these 18 additional places: Pomona, California (71 percent); Norwalk, California (70 percent); Miami, Florida (70 percent); El Monte, California (69 percent); Ontario, California (69 percent); Fontana, California (67 percent); San Antonio, Texas (63 percent); Pasadena, Texas (62 percent); San Bernardino, California (60 percent); Corpus Christi, Texas (60 percent); Elizabeth, New Jersey (59 percent); Chula Vista, California (58 percent); Paterson, New Jersey (58 percent); Palmdale, California (54 percent); Moreno Valley, California (54 percent); West Covina, California (53 percent); Anaheim, California (53 percent); and Inglewood, California (51 percent).

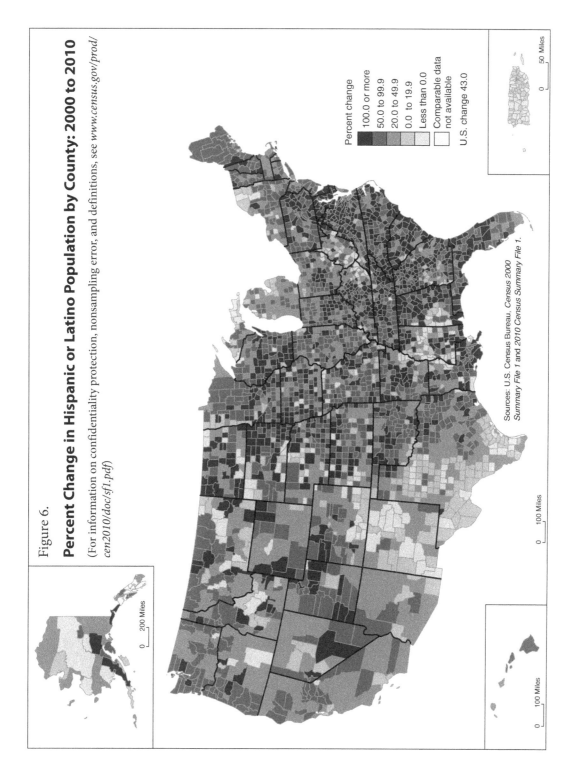

Figure 6.

Percent Change in Hispanic or Latino Population by County: 2000 to 2010

(For information on confidentiality protection, nonsampling error, and definitions, see *www.census.gov/prod/cen2010/doc/sf1.pdf*)

Percent change

- 100.0 or more
- 50.0 to 99.9
- 20.0 to 49.9
- 0.0 to 19.9
- Less than 0.0
- Comparable data not available

U.S. change 43.0

Sources: U.S. Census Bureau, *Census 2000 Summary File 1* and *2010 Census Summary File 1*.

Table 5.
Ten Places With the Highest Number and Percentage of Hispanics or Latinos: 2010
(For information on confidentiality protection, nonsampling error, and definitions, see *www.census.gov/prod/cen2010/doc/sf1.pdf*)

Place	Total population	Hispanic or Latino population	
		Rank	Number
NUMBER			
New York, NY.	8,175,133	1	2,336,076
Los Angeles, CA	3,792,621	2	1,838,822
Houston, TX.	2,099,451	3	919,668
San Antonio, TX.	1,327,407	4	838,952
Chicago, IL	2,695,598	5	778,862
Phoenix, AZ.	1,445,632	6	589,877
El Paso, TX	649,121	7	523,721
Dallas, TX	1,197,816	8	507,309
San Diego, CA.	1,307,402	9	376,020
San Jose, CA.	945,942	10	313,636

Place[1]	Total population	Rank	Percent of total population
PERCENT			
East Los Angeles, CA[2]	126,496	1	97.1
Laredo, TX.	236,091	2	95.6
Hialeah, FL	224,669	3	94.7
Brownsville, TX	175,023	4	93.2
McAllen, TX.	129,877	5	84.6
El Paso, TX	649,121	6	80.7
Santa Ana, CA.	324,528	7	78.2
Salinas, CA	150,441	8	75.0
Oxnard, CA	197,899	9	73.5
Downey, CA.	111,772	10	70.7

[1] Places of 100,000 or more total population. The 2010 Census showed 282 places in the United States with 100,000 or more population. They included 273 incorporated places (including 5 consolidated cities) and 9 census designated places that were not legally incorporated.

[2] East Los Angeles, CA, is a census designated place and is not legally incorporated.

Source: U.S. Census Bureau, *2010 Census Summary File 1.*

ADDITIONAL FINDINGS ON THE HISPANIC POPULATION

The Hispanic population predominantly identified as either "White" or "Some Other Race"

People of Hispanic origin may be of any race. Starting in 1997, OMB required federal agencies to use a minimum of five race categories: White, Black or African American, American Indian or Alaska Native, Asian, and Native Hawaiian or Other Pacific Islander. For respondents unable to identify with any of these five race categories, OMB approved the Census

Bureau's inclusion of a sixth category—Some Other Race—on the Census 2000 and 2010 Census questionnaires.[19]

For the 2010 Census, a new instruction was added immediately preceding the questions on Hispanic origin and race, which was not used in Census 2000. The instruction stated that "For this census, Hispanic origins are not races" because in the federal statistical system, Hispanic origin is considered to be a separate concept from race. However, this did not preclude individuals from self-identifying their race as "Latino," "Mexican," "Puerto Rican," "Salvadoran," or other national origins or ethnicities; in fact, many did so. If the response provided to the race question could not be classified in one or more of the five OMB race groups, it was generally classified in the category Some Other Race. Therefore, responses to the question on race that reflect a Hispanic origin were classified in the Some Other Race category.

The 2010 Census racial distributions of the Hispanic population are shown in Table 6. In 2010, 94 percent of Hispanic respondents (47.4 million) reported one race.[20] Over half (53 percent) of the Hispanic population identified as White and no other race, while about one-third (37 percent) provided responses that were classified as Some Other Race alone when responding to the question on race. Much smaller proportions of Hispanics identified as other race groups alone: Black alone (2 percent), American Indian and Alaska Native alone (1 percent), Asian alone (0.4 percent), and Native Hawaiian and Other Pacific Islander alone (0.1 percent). About 3 million Hispanics (6 percent) reported multiple races. Among Hispanics who reported multiple races, a large proportion reported race combinations involving Some Other Race.

The racial distribution of the Mexican origin population was similar to the distribution of the total Hispanic population. Mexicans also reported predominantly as White alone (53 percent) and Some Other Race alone (39 percent). Mexicans were less likely to report as Black alone (1 percent) than the total Hispanic population.

On the other hand, the racial distribution of other Central American groups was different than that of the total Hispanic population. People of Guatemalan and Salvadoran origin were less likely to report as White alone (about 40 percent for both groups), more likely to report as only Some Other Race (about 50 percent for both), and more likely to report multiple races (about 7 percent for both). Also, Guatemalans were more likely to report as American Indian and Alaska Native alone (3 percent). Respondents that reported

---

[19] For more information on the 2010 Census race question, see *Overview of Race and Hispanic Origin: 2010* at <www.census.gov/prod/cen2010/briefs/c2010br-02.pdf>.

[20] Individuals who responded to the question on race by indicating only one race are referred to as the *race-alone* population or the group that reported only one race category. Six categories make up this population: White alone, Black or African American alone, American Indian and Alaska Native alone, Asian alone, Native Hawaiian and Other Pacific Islander alone, and Some Other Race alone. Individuals who chose more than 1 of the 6 race categories are referred to as the Two or More Races population. All respondents who indicated more than one race can be collapsed into the Two or More Races category which, combined with the six race-alone categories, yields seven mutually exclusive and exhaustive categories. Thus, the six race-alone categories and the Two or More Races category sum to the total population.

Table 6.
Hispanic or Latino Population by Type of Origin and Race: 2010
(For information on confidentiality protection, nonsampling error, and definitions, see www.census.gov/prod/cen2010/doc/sf1.pdf)

Origin	Total Hispanic or Latino population	One Race							Two or More Races
		Total	White	Black or African American	American Indian and Alaska Native	Asian	Native Hawaiian and Other Pacific Islander	Some Other Race	
NUMBER									
Total Hispanic	50,477,594	47,435,002	26,735,713	1,243,471	685,150	209,128	58,437	18,503,103	3,042,592
Central American.	35,796,538	33,920,977	18,491,777	425,389	523,432	113,846	34,096	14,332,437	1,875,561
Mexican	31,798,258	30,221,886	16,794,111	296,778	460,098	101,654	24,600	12,544,645	1,576,372
Guatemalan	1,044,209	969,462	401,763	11,471	31,197	2,386	7,251	515,394	74,747
Salvadoran.	1,648,968	1,535,703	663,224	16,150	17,682	4,737	1,105	832,805	113,265
Other Central American[1]	1,305,103	1,193,926	632,679	100,990	14,455	5,069	1,140	439,593	111,177
South American[2]	2,769,434	2,587,683	1,825,468	37,786	21,053	12,224	1,079	690,073	181,751
Caribbean	7,823,966	7,217,371	4,400,071	667,775	64,689	32,759	12,814	2,039,263	606,595
Cuban	1,785,547	1,719,585	1,525,521	82,398	3,002	4,391	774	103,499	65,962
Dominican	1,414,703	1,276,878	419,016	182,005	19,183	4,056	1,279	651,339	137,825
Puerto Rican	4,623,716	4,220,908	2,455,534	403,372	42,504	24,312	10,761	1,284,425	402,808
All other Hispanic[3]	4,087,656	3,708,971	2,018,397	112,521	75,976	50,299	10,448	1,441,330	378,685
PERCENT									
Total Hispanic	100.0	94.0	53.0	2.5	1.4	0.4	0.1	36.7	6.0
Central American.	100.0	94.8	51.7	1.2	1.5	0.3	0.1	40.0	5.2
Mexican	100.0	95.0	52.8	0.9	1.4	0.3	0.1	39.5	5.0
Guatemalan	100.0	92.8	38.5	1.1	3.0	0.2	0.7	49.4	7.2
Salvadoran.	100.0	93.1	40.2	1.0	1.1	0.3	0.1	50.5	6.9
Other Central American[1]	100.0	91.5	48.5	7.7	1.1	0.4	0.1	33.7	8.5
South American[2]	100.0	93.4	65.9	1.4	0.8	0.4	–	24.9	6.6
Caribbean	100.0	92.2	56.2	8.5	0.8	0.4	0.2	26.1	7.8
Cuban	100.0	96.3	85.4	4.6	0.2	0.2	–	5.8	3.7
Dominican	100.0	90.3	29.6	12.9	1.4	0.3	0.1	46.0	9.7
Puerto Rican	100.0	91.3	53.1	8.7	0.9	0.5	0.2	27.8	8.7
All other Hispanic[3]	100.0	90.7	49.4	2.8	1.9	1.2	0.3	35.3	9.3

– Percentage rounds to 0.0

[1] This category includes people who reported "Costa Rican," "Honduran," "Nicaraguan," "Panamanian," Central American Indian groups, "Canal Zone," and "Central American."

[2] This category includes people who reported "Argentinean," "Bolivian," "Chilean," "Colombian," "Ecuadorian," "Paraguayan," "Peruvian," "Uruguayan," "Venezuelan," South American Indian groups, and "South American."

[3] This category includes people who reported "Spaniard," as well as "Hispanic" or "Latino" and other general terms.

Source: U.S. Census Bureau, 2010 Census special tabulation.

as Other Central American were less likely to report as White alone (48 percent), more likely to report as Black alone (8 percent), less likely to report as Some Other Race alone (34 percent), and more likely to report multiple races (9 percent).

South American Hispanics also reported largely as White alone and Some Other Race alone but at proportions much different than the total Hispanic population. South American Hispanics were more likely to report as White only (about two-thirds) and less likely to report only as Some Other Race (about one-quarter) than the total Hispanic population.

Respondents of Cuban origin were much more likely than the total Hispanic population to report as White alone (85 percent), more likely to report as Black alone (5 percent), less likely to report as Some Other Race alone (6 percent), and less likely to report as multiple races (4 percent). Dominicans were much less likely to report as White alone (30 percent), much more likely to report as Black alone (13 percent), more likely to report as Some Other Race alone (46 percent), and more likely to report as multiple races (10 percent). Puerto Ricans were more likely to report as Black alone (9 percent), less likely to report as Some Other Race alone (28 percent), and more likely to report multiple races (9 percent). About half of all other Hispanics reported as White alone and about one-third provided responses classified as Some Other Race alone. All other Hispanics were slightly more likely to report as Black alone (3 percent), more likely to report as American Indian and Alaska Native alone (2 percent), more likely to report as Asian alone (1 percent), slightly more likely to report as Native Hawaiian and Other Pacific Islander alone (0.3 percent), and more likely to report as multiple races (9 percent).

SUMMARY

This report presented data from the 2010 Census that illustrated the nation's changing ethnic diversity. The Hispanic population accounted for over half the growth of the total population in the United States between 2000 and 2010. The examination of ethnic group distributions nationally shows that the Mexican population is still numerically and proportionally the largest Hispanic group in the United States. Although Mexicans were the largest Hispanic group, they grew at a rate slower than many of the other detailed Hispanic groups.

Racial classification issues continue to persist among those who identify as Hispanic, resulting in a substantial proportion of that population being categorized as Some Other Race. Geographically, there are a number of areas, particularly in the Western and Southern parts of the United States that have large proportions of the Hispanic population. Overall, the U.S. population has become more ethnically diverse over time. Throughout the decade, the Census Bureau will release additional information on Hispanic origin population groups, which will provide more insights into the nation's ethnic diversity.

ABOUT THE 2010 CENSUS

Why was the 2010 Census conducted?

The U.S. Constitution mandates that a census be taken in the United States every 10 years. This is required in order to determine the number of seats each state is to receive in the U.S. House of Representatives.

Why did the 2010 Census ask the question on Hispanic origin?

The Census Bureau collects data on Hispanic origin and race to fulfill a variety of legislative and program requirements. Data on Hispanic origin and race are used in the legislative redistricting process carried out by the states and in monitoring local jurisdictions' compliance with the Voting Rights Act. More broadly, data on Hispanic origin are critical for research that underlies many policy decisions at all levels of government.

How do data from the question on Hispanic origin benefit me, my family, and my community?

All levels of government need information on Hispanic origin to implement and evaluate programs, or enforce laws, such as the Civil Rights Act, Voting Rights Act, Fair Housing Act, Equal Employment Opportunity Act, and the 2010 Census Redistricting Data Program. Both public and private organizations use Hispanic origin information to find areas where groups may need special services and to plan and implement education, housing, health, and other programs that address these needs. For example, a school system might use this information to design cultural activities that reflect the diversity in their community. Or a business could use it to select the mix of merchandise it will sell in a new store. Census information also helps identify areas where residents might need services of particular importance to certain ethnic groups, such as screening for hypertension or diabetes.

FOR MORE INFORMATION

For more information on race and Hispanic origin in the United States, visit the Census Bureau's Internet site at <www.census.gov/population/www/socdemo/hispanic/hispanic.html> and <www.census.gov/population/www/socdemo/race/race.html>.

Data on Hispanic origin and race from the *2010 Census Summary File 1* are released on a state-by-state basis. For a detailed schedule of 2010 Census products and release dates, visit <www.census.gov/population/www/cen2010/glance/index.html>. For more information on confidentiality protection, nonsampling error, and definitions, see <www.census.gov/prod/cen2010/doc/sf1.pdf>.

For more information on specific race and ethnic groups in the United States, go to <www.census.gov/> and click on "Minority Links." This Web page includes information about the 2010 Census and provides links to reports based on past censuses and surveys focusing on the social and economic characteristics of the Hispanic or Latino, Black or African American, American Indian and Alaska Native, Asian, and Native Hawaiian and Other Pacific Islander populations.

Information on other population and housing topics is presented in the 2010 Census Briefs series, located on the Census Bureau's Web site at <www.census.gov/prod/cen2010/>.

This series presents information about race, Hispanic origin, age, sex, household type, housing tenure, and people who reside in group quarters.

For more information about the 2010 Census, including data products, call the Customer Services Center at 1-800-923-8282. You can also visit the Census Bureau's Question and Answer Center at <ask.census.gov> to submit your question online.

NOTES

Chapter 2

[1] Eric R. Wolf, *Sons of the Shaking Earth* (Chicago: University of Chicago Press, 1959), p. 23.

[2] José Antonio Burciaga, *Drink Cultura: Chicanismo* (Santa Barbara: Joshua Odell, 1993), pp. 41, 44.

[3] Ignacio Bernal, *The Olmec World* (Berkeley: University of California Press, 1969), p. 17.

[4] John Noble Wilford, *New York Times,* September 15, 2006.

[5] Ignacio Bernal, *The Olmec World* (Berkeley: University of California Press, 1969), p. 193.

[6] Michael C. Meyer, William L. Sherman, and Susan M. Deeds, *The Course of Mexican History* (New York: Oxford University Press, 1999), pp. 82, 83, 85.

[7] Miguel León-Portilla, *Aztec Thought and Culture* (Norman: University of Oklahoma Press, 1963), pp. 4, 5, 7.

Chapter 3

[1] Ignacio Bernal, *Mexico Before Cortez: Art, History, and Legend* (New York: Anchor Press, 1963), p. 128.

[2] José Antonio Burciaga, *Drink Cultura: Chicanismo* (Santa Barbara: Joshua Odell, 1993), p. 57.

[3] Michael C. Meyer, William L. Sherman, and Susan M. Deeds, *The Course of Mexican History* (New York: Oxford University Press, 1999), p. 206.

[4] Carey McWilliams, *North from Mexico* (New York: Praeger, 1948), pp. 43, 44.

Chapter 4

[1] Allen R. Myerson, New Times, *A New Look at Those Alamo Stories.* (New York Times) March 29, 1994.

[2] Glenn W. Price, *Origins of the War with Mexico* (Austin: University of Texas Press, 1967), p. 18.

[3] Ibid., p. 158.

[4] Ibid., p. 89.

[5] Archie P. McDonald, *The Mexican War: Crisis for American Democracy* (Lexington, MA: D. C. Heath and Company, 1969,) p. 49.

[6] Glenn W. Price, op. cit., p. 17.

[7] Norman A. Graebner, *Empire of the Pacific* (New York: The Roland Press Company, 1955), p. 218.

[8] Feliciano Rivera, *A Mexican American Source Book* (Menlo Park, CA: Educational Consulting Associates, 1970), pp. 184–186.

[9] Ibid.

[10] Leonard Pitt, *The Decline of the Californios* (Berkeley: University of California Press, 1968), pp. 85–86, 103.

[11] Carey McWilliams, *North from Mexico* (New York: Greenwood Press, 1968), pp. 112–113.

[12] *Feliciano* Rivera, op. cit.

Chapter 5

[1] Carey McWilliams, *North from Mexico* (New York: Praeger, 1948), p. 77

[2] Ibid., pp. 85, 102.

[3] José Antonio Burciaga, *Drink Cultura: Chicanismo* (Santa Barbara: Joshua Odell, 1993), pp. 127, 128.

[4] Américo Paredes, *With a Pistol in His Hand: A Border Ballad and Its Hero* (Austin: University of Texas Press, 1958).

Chapter 6

[1] Carey McWilliams, *North from Mexico* (New York: Praeger, 1948), p. 109.

[2] Ibid., p. 188.

Chapter 7

[1] Ralph Ellison, *Invisible Man* (New York: Random House, 1952).

[2] Interview with Ms. Dolores Huerta. May 1, 2008, Fresno, California.

REFERENCES

Acuna, Rodolfo. *Occupied America: A History of Chicanos.* 2004. New York: Harper & Row.

Bernal, Ignacio. *Mexico before Cortez: Art, History, and Legend.* 1975. Garden City, NY: Anchor Press/ Doubleday.

Bernal, Ignacio. *The Olmec World.* 1969. Berkeley: University of California Press.

Brenner, Anita, and George R. Leighton. *The Wind That Swept Mexico: The History of the Mexican Revolution of 1910–1942.* 1971. Austin: University of Texas Press.

Burciaga, Jose Antonio. *Drink Cultura: Chicanismo.* 1993. Santa Barbara: Joshua Odell Editions.

Burns, E. Bradford. *Latin America: A Concise Interpretive History.* 2002. Upper Saddle River, NJ: Pearson Education.

California state profile (2016). Retrieved from http://www.ballotpedia.org

Carmack, Robert M. *The Legacy of Mesoamerica: History and Culture of a Native American Civilization.* 2007. Upper Saddle River, NJ: Pearson Education.

Castro, M.J. (1998, August). Bilingual education and Proposition 227: What really happened? Retrieved from http://www.languagepolicy.net

Cockcroft, James D. *Intellectual Precursors of the Mexican Revolution 1900–1913.* 1968. Austin: University of Texas Press.

English learner (EL) students who are Hispanic/Latino. (2015, October). Retrieved from http://www.ed.gov.olea

Evans, Susan Toby. *Ancient Mexico & Central America: Archaeology and Culture History.* 2004. New York: Thames & Hudson.

Facts about English learners in California—CalEdFacts. (2015, September 21). Retrieved from http://www.cde.ca.gov/ds/sd/cb/cefelfacts.asp

Fingertip facts on education in California—CalEdFacts. (2015, September 15). Retrieved from http://www.cde.ca.gov/ds/sd/cb/ceffingertipfacts.asp

Forbes, Jack D. *Aztecas Del Norte: The Chicanos of Aztlan.* 1973. Greenwich, CT: Fawcett Publications.

Griswold del Castillo, Richard. *The Treaty of Guadalupe Hidalgo: A Legacy of Conflict.* 1990. Norman: University of Oklahoma Press.

Griswold del Castillo, Richard. *La Familia: Chicano Families in the Urban Southwest 1848 to the Present.* 1984. Notre Dame, IN: University of Notre Dame Press.

Hayes-Bautista, David E. *La Nueva California: Latinos in the Golden State.* 2004. Berkeley: University of California Press.

Kim, C. (2013). Lost American DREAM of undocumented students: Understanding the DREAM (Development, Relief, and Education for Alien Minors) Act. *Children & Schools*, 35(1), 55–58.

Leon-Portilla, Miguel. *Aztec Thought and Culture.* 1963. Norman: University of Oklahoma Press.

Love, Bruce. *The Paris Codex: Handbook for a Maya Priest.* 1994. Austin: University of Texas Press.

Madrid, M. (2008). The unheralded history of the Lemon Grove desegregation case. *Multicultural Education* (Spring, 2008), 15–19.

Mazon, Mauricio. *The Zoot-Suit Riots: The Psychology of Symbolic Annihilation.* 1984. Austin: University of Texas Press.

McDonald, Archie P. *The Mexican War: Crisis for American Democracy.* 1969. Lexington, MA: D.C. Heath.

McWilliams, Carey. *North from Mexico: The Spanish-Speaking People of the United States.* 1990. New York: Praeger Publishers.

Meyer, Michael C., William L. Sherman, and Susan M. Deeds. *The Course of Mexican History.* 1999. New York: Oxford University Press.

Montemayor, Robert, and Henry Mendoza. *Right before Our Eyes: Latinos Past, Present and Future.* 2004. Tempe, AZ: Scholargy Publishing.

Morin, Raul. *Among the Valiant, Mexican Americans in WWII and Korea.* 1963. Los Angeles, CA: Border Publishing.

Overview of race and Hispanic origin: 2010. (2011, March). Retrieved from http://www.census.gov

Paredes, Américo. *With a Pistol in His Hand: A Border Ballad and Its Hero.* 1958. Austin: University of Texas Press.

Peterson, Fredrick A. *Ancient Mexico: An Introduction to the Pre-Hispanic Cultures.* 1962. New York: Capricorn Books.

Pitt, Leonard. *The Decline of the Californios: A Social History of the Spanish-Speaking Californians, 1846–1890.* 1971. Berkeley: University of California Press.

Price, Glenn W. *Origins of the War with Mexico: The Polk-Stockton Intrigue.* 1967. Austin: University of Texas Press.

Rendon, Armando B. *Chicano Manifesto: The History and Aspiration of the Second Largest Minority in America.* 1971. New York: Collier Macmillan. Ruiz, Ramon Eduardo. *The Mexican War: Was It Manifest Destiny?* 1963. New York: Hold, Rinehart & Winston.

Spring, J. (2010). *American education* (14th ed). New York, NY: McGraw-Hill, Higher Education.

Tatum, Charles M. *Chicano Popular Culture: Que Hable El Pueblo.* 2001. Tucson: University of Arizona Press.

Taube, Karl. *Aztec and Maya Myths: The Legendary Past.* 1997. Austin: University of Texas.

Trujillo, Charley. *Soldados: Chicanos in Vietnam.* 1990. San Jose, CA: Chusma House Publications.

Wolf, Eric. *Sons of the Shaking Earth.* 1959. Chicago: University of Chicago Press.

GLOSSARY

with Names, Events, and Locations

Acculturation   Interaction between cultures permits a two-way process of cultural sharing, exchange, and influence. Therefore, Latinos may become acculturated to American society and nonetheless maintain, preserve, and foster Latino culture.

Acosta, Oscar Zeta   Author and Chicano Movement lawyer; also known as *The Brown Buffalo*.

Alamo   An old mission located in San Antonio, Texas. Anglo Americans rebelled against México and were confronted by General Santa Anna in the Battle of the Alamo during the Texas Revolution.

Alurista   A Chicano poet associated with the Chicano Movement.

American GI Forum   An organization that focuses on veterans' issues, civil rights, and education.

Anáhuac   Valley of Anáhuac refers to an ancient name for the valley of México where the Azteca-Mexica established their empire.

Anaya, Rodolfo   Author of novels such as *Bless Me Ultima*.

Ancient American civilizations   Referring to the indigenous people in the Américas before Columbus.

Anzaldúa, Gloria   Chicana author of *Borderlands/La Frontera: The New Mestiza*.

Assimilation   A process whereby a member of an ethnic racial minority group acquires behaviors, lifestyles, values, and language of the dominant ethnic racial majority group. Thus, Latinos become Americanized in this assimilation process.

Azteca   The civilization in central México conquered by the Spanish in 1519. Also known as Mexica.

Aztec Calendar   More accurately known as the *Sun Stone*, it is the greatest book of the Américas telling the story of the indigenous peoples.

Aztlán   According to legend, the ancestral homeland of the Azteca-Mexica. The Chicano Movement declared the location to be the Southwestern United States.

Baca, Elfego   Known in Texas as a social bandit and legendary folk hero (born in New Mexico).

Baca, Judith F.   Chicana muralist famous for the Great Wall of Los Angeles.

Barrios/Colonias   Urban *barrios* and rural *colonias* are culturally cohesive districts, neighborhoods, and communities.

Battle of San Jacinto   A battle where General Santa Anna was captured by Sam Houston and forced to sign the Treaty of Velasco. It recognized Texas as being independent from México.

Bering Strait   The narrow section of ocean that separates Asia from Alaska.

Bicultural   When an individual acquires values, behaviors, and traits of two cultural groups.

Bilingual   The ability to communicate in two languages.

Bilingual Education   An educational program where second language learners are taught in their primary language and then transitioned to English.

Border Patrol   ICE, Immigration and Customs Enforcement. Customs and Border Protection is a federal law enforcement agency of the U.S. Department of Homeland Security that is responsible for immigration and border enforcement. This was formerly known to Latinos as the INS or *La Migra*.

Burciaga, José Antonio   Chicano author and artist known for many works, including *The Last Supper of Chicano Heroes*.

California Gold Rush, 1848   Discovery of gold in California. Mexicans and other Latino Americanos were first on the scene providing their gold mining tools and techniques.

California missions   The Spanish priests established a mission system and gathered in the local Indians in the territory of northern New Spain. It later became northern México, and afterwards the Southwest of the United States.

Castro, Sal   The teacher that inspired students during the 1968 high school walkouts in Los Angeles protesting education inequities and discrimination.

Catholicism   The Christian religion that was brought to the Américas with the Spanish conquerors.

Chávez, César   Founder of the United Farm Workers, labor leader, and civil rights/human rights activist.

Chicano/Chicana   A name, term, and label popularized by the Chicano Movement referring to Mexican Americans involved in *El Movimiento* fighting for *La Causa*.

Chicano Moratorium   A Chicano march protesting social injustice and the Viet Nam War through the streets of East Los Angeles on August 29, 1970. This march for social justice is commemorated every year.

Chicano Movement   Also known as *El Movimiento.* Began in the 1960s with the goal of achieving social justice, equality, civil rights, human rights, and empowerment.

Chichén-Itza   A major pre-Columbian archaeological site of the Maya located in the state of Yucatán.

Chinampas   "Floating Gardens." Used by the Azteca to grow crops on shallow lake beds in the Valley of México.

Cinco de Mayo   A cultural celebration commemorating the Mexican victory over the French in the Battle of Puebla. Afterwards, the French invasion continued and France occupied México. This battle had implications for France and the American Civil War.

© IgorGolovniov, 2013. Used under license from Shutterstock, Inc.

Cisneros, Sandra   Prolific Chicana author.

Colonial México   Refers to the Spanish colony that became México after Mexican Independence.

Columbus, Christopher   A colonizer, navigator, explorer, and a precursor of the Spanish colonization of the Américas.

Copán   A major pre-Columbian archeological site of the Maya civilization located in Honduras.

Cortés, Hernán   The Spanish *conquistador* of the Aztec Empire and the leader instrumental in the colonization of the Américas.

Cortéz, Gregorio   Known in Texas as a social bandit and legendary folk hero.

Cortina, Juan "Cheno"   Known in Texas as a social bandit and legendary folk hero.

Corona, Bert   A major leader in the Mexican American Political Association and also the Chicano Movement.

Criollos   Those of pure Spanish blood born in New Spain.

CSO   The Community Service Organization taught activists to organize the community to improve their social conditions. César Chávez and Dolores Huerta worked with the CSO before forming the United Farm Workers.

Cuauhtémoc   The last Azteca ruler in 1521, whose name means "one that has descended like an eagle."

Cuitláhuac   The Azteca king in 1520; was ruler between the rule of Moctezuma and Cuauhtémoc.

Cultural pluralism   The existence of diverse cultures coexisting together in one society.

Culture   Patterns of human activity and symbolic structures that give activities significance and importance. This includes customs, traditions, rituals, celebrations, and other cultural behaviors. Culture includes: Attitudes, behaviors, values and beliefs.

Curanderismo   The art and science of health and medicine from an indigenous cultural traditional perspective.

Día de la Revolución   The day celebrating the Mexican Revolution of 1910; November 20 of each year.

Día de la Virgen de Guadalupe   A religious celebration on December 12 of each year.

Día de las Madres   In México Mother's Day is celebrated on May 10 of each year.

Día de los Muertos   A holiday to remember and honor the deceased. Day of the Dead is a celebration of death as an extension of life. This celebration combines indigenous beliefs with the Catholic All Saints and All Souls Days (November 1 and 2).

Día de Los Santos Reyes   Celebrated on January 6. In México people exchange presents to celebrate the arrival of the three wise men bearing gifts for baby Jesus Christ.

Diego, Juan   An indigenous man claiming to see an apparition of the Virgin Mary known as *La Virgen de Guadalupe*. This had a significant impact on the spread of Catholicism in New Spain.

Discrimination   A negative behavior or action against an individual or group. Discrimination is generally due to national, cultural, ethnic, racial, religious, gender, or other differences.

Domestication of plants   Plants cultivated by humans.

Doña Marina/La Malinche   An indigenous woman who accompanied Hernán Cortés and played a very important role as his interpreter, informant, and mistress. She is an intriguing cultural symbol in folklore and literature.

Dual Immersion Education   An educational program where all subjects are taught in a primary language such as Spanish, then gradually transitioned to Spanish/English. The population of students is ethnically and racially mixed. Parents usually make a commitment to continue their children in the program and by twelfth grade students are fully bilingual.

El Grito de Dolores   The battle cry starting the Mexican war of independence in the town of Dolores. September 16 is celebrated as Mexican Independence Day.

El Teatro Campesino   Theatrical troupe founded by Luis Valdez as an arm of the United Farm Workers.

Esparza, Moctezuma   Film director who co-produced *Selena* (1997) with Gregory Nava. He is also known for the production of *The Ballet of Gregorio Cortez* (1982), *The Milagro Beanfield War* (1988), and the HBO movie, *WalkOut* (2006).

Ethnocentrism   To be ethnocentric. The belief that one's social and cultural group is better or superior.

Gonzalez, Rodolfo "Corky"   A Chicano boxer, poet, political activist, and one of the founders of the Chicano Movement. He is the author of the epic Chicano poem, *I Am Joaquín*.

Great Depression   A dramatic economic downturn during the 1930s associated with the stock market crash of 1929.

Gutiérrez, José Ángel   Founder of La Raza Unida Party and major leader in the Chicano Movement.

Hacienda   A Spanish word for a large estate and/or a ranch.

Hacienda System   A system of large land-holdings and estates owned by landlords or *hacendados*.

Hidalgo, Miguel   A Mexican Roman Catholic priest; revolutionary leader known for the famous *El Grito de Dolores* during period of Mexican independence from Spain.

Hispanic   Refers to the culture of Spanish-speaking people. This term has been promulgated and popularized by the U.S. government and American society.

Huerta, Dolores   Cofounder of the United Farm Workers of America and community activist.

Illegal alien   From the Chicano-Latino perspective this is a derogatory and offensive term; *Mexicanos* are the indigenous people of Aztlán.

Inca   The largest pre-Columbian civilization; their empire stretched most of the Pacific coast of South America.

Indigenous   The first original settlers who inhabit a geographic region.

Juárez, Benito   A Zapotec Indian and beloved president of México.

Kahlo, Frida   A famous Mexican painter married to the also famous Diego Rivera. Her self-portraits often expressed her pain and sexuality.

La Cuaresma   The Easter religious season of Lent.

La Causa   Literally means *the Cause*. This motto represents the Chicano-Chicana fight for social justice and equality.

La Navidad   The Christmas season as represented by the birth of Jesus Christ and the nativity scene.

La Noche Triste   This was the night during the Spanish Conquest when the Spanish were nearly annihilated and barely escaped the Azteca.

La Raza   A term used with pride, honor, and dignity referring to a race of people blending the Spanish with the indigenous cultures.

La Raza Unida Party   A Chicano political party active in the early 1970s.

L'Archeveque, Sostenes   Known in New México as a social bandit and legendary folk hero.

Las Posadas   The Christmas season as represented by the story of Mary and Joseph seeking lodging.

Latino   An umbrella term for persons in the United States with cultural roots in México or Latino América.

La Virgen de Guadalupe   A Roman Catholic icon depicted as an apparition of the Virgin Mary; Mexico's beloved religious and cultural image.

Los Niños Héroes   At the battle of Chapultepec Castle, six teenage Mexican cadets fought to their death rather than surrender to the invading U.S. forces. The last cadet died by wrapping himself in the Mexican flag and leaping from the castle as a symbolic gesture of resistance. Their names: Juan de la Barrera; Juan Escutia; Francisco Márquez; Augustín Melgar; Fernando Montes de Oca; Vicente Suárez. Juan Escutia was the cadet that fell to his death rather than surrendering the Mexican flag. Commemorated on September 13 of each year.

Los Tres Grandes   *The Three Great Ones* refers to the Mexican master painters, Diego Rivera, José Clemente Orozco, and David Alfaro Siqueiros.

LULAC   League of United Latin American Citizens, a community organization.

Madero, Francisco   Politician, writer, revolutionary, and president of México during the Mexican Revolution of 1910.

MALDEF   Mexican American Legal Defense and Education Fund, a nonprofit civil rights organization formed to protect Latino legal rights in the United States.

Manifest Destiny   The belief that the United States was destined to expand from the Atlantic to the Pacific Ocean.

MAPA   Mexican American Political Association is a community organization formed to promote the social and political interests of Mexican Americans in the United States.

Maya   A great Mesoamerican civilization in pre-Columbian América.

MEChA   A Chicano-Chicana student organization of activists promoting social justice and educational equality and opportunity.

Melting pot process   The theoretical process whereby members of a minority group melt and become absorbed into the culture and society of the majority group. Thus, Latinos may become Americanized in an assimilation process and melt into the cultural mainstream of American society.

Mestizo/Mezcla/Mestizaje   Terms used to designate people of mixed Spanish and Indian blood and culture.

Mestizo culture   The combination and blending of the Spanish and indigenous cultures.

Mexica   Azteca-Mexica is the more accurate name for the indigenous people that ruled the Azteca Empire.

Mexican-American War 1846–1848   A military conflict and intervention by the United States related to *manifest destiny* and President James K. Polk. As a result, the United States acquired what became the Southwest, from Texas to California.

Mexican Independence   The period between 1810 and 1821; the war of independence from Spain.

Mexican Independence Day   Celebrated September 16 commemorating the independence movement from Spain.

Mexican Revolution of 1910   A major armed struggle and civil war led by Francisco Madero and other revolutionaries against President Porfirio Díaz and the ruling class.

Moctezuma II   Aztec ruler from 1502 to 1520; also known as Moctezuma Xocoyótzin.

Murrieta, Joaquín   Known in California as a social bandit and legendary folk hero.

Nava, Gregory   Film director of movies such as *El Norte* and *My Family/Mi Familia*. He co-produced *Selena* (1997) with Moctezuma Esparza.

Noriega, Chon   Film critic and expert on Chicano-Latino cinema.

Nueva España, New Spain   The territory colonized by Spain. The territory ranged from today's Florida, to the Midwest, to California and south to the tip of South America (with the exception of Brazil).

Olmeca   Ancient pre-Columbian people of Central México expanding from today's Vera Cruz; known as *La Cultura Madre*.

Olmos, Edward James   Mexican American actor, director and producer. Starred in movies such as *Zoot Suit* (1981); *Stand and Deliver* (1988); *American Me* (1992); *My Family* (1995); *Selena* (1997).

Pachucos/Pachucas   Mexican American youth that developed their own subculture during the 1940s; wore their own distinctive zoot suit clothes and developed a dialect known as *pachuquismo*.

Palenque   A major pre-Columbian archeological site of the Maya civilization located in the state of Chiapas.

Paredes, Américo   Chicano scholar and author of *With this Pistol in His Hand: A Border Ballad and Its Hero.*

Polk, James K.   The eleventh president of the United States; declared war on México in 1846.

Pre-Columbian América   Refers to the Américas before the appearance of Columbus and the Europeans.

Pre-Hispanic América   Refers to the Américas before the appearance of the Spanish.

Prejudice   A prejudgment and negative attitude based on generalizations about a group.

Quetzalcóatl   The king of the Tolteca at the city of Tula; a major deity throughout ancient central México; also known as the Feathered Serpent and Kukulcán.

Quinceañera   A unique celebration for a young woman's fifteenth birthday. In the *old* traditional culture, this was a religious rite of passage celebrating the girl entering womanhood; she was thus available for courtship and marriage.

Racism   Prejudice and discrimination based on race and institutionalized into the society. This is known as institutionalized racism.

Religious syncretism   The attempt to reconcile and synchronize contradictory beliefs in religion. For example, the indigenous people attempted to synchronize their belief system with the Christianity of the Spanish.

Rivera, Diego   A world-famous Mexican painter and husband to Frida Kahlo.

Saint Patrick's Battalion   During the Mexican-American War, the San Patricios joined the Mexican army fighting to protect México against the invading U.S. military. The epic story of these Irish Catholic soldiers is remembered on St. Patrick's Day for their courage and bravery.

Salazar, Rubén   A Mexican American journalist killed by the police during the march called the Chicano Moratorium in East Los Angeles on August 29, 1970.

Salinas, Omar   Luis Omar Salinas was a Chicano poet from the San Joaquín Valley in California.

Santa Anna (General)   Antonio López de Santa Anna was a Mexican political leader and president of México during the 1800s.

Sí Se Puede!   This was a powerful motto coined by Dolores Huerta used to motivate people in the struggle for farmworker social justice and equality.

Sor Juana Inéz de la Cruz   The greatest Mexican writer of the Colonial era; wrote about women's rights and freedom. She combined feminism and romance in her poetry and resided as a nun in a convent.

Spanish Conquest   Spain's invasion and conquest of the Azteca-Mexica; subsequent settlement and rule over what later became Nueva España then Latino América.

Spanish land grants   Land claims by Spanish and Mestizo settlers during the time of New Spain.

Tajín   A pre-Columbian archaeological site of the Maya civilization located in the state of Veracruz.

Tehuacán   Valley of Tehuacán refers to an indigenous settlement known for the earliest domestication of corn.

Tejano   A term used by *Mexicanos* that are born and living in the state of Texas.

Tejano music   Some authorities on the history of music in the United States consider Texas as pivotal in the development and evolution of Mexican American music.

Tejas   Mexican Tejas; the region that is now Texas.

Tenochtitlán   The capital of the Azteca Empire, which is today buried under México City.

Teotihuacán   The pre-Columbian city of the Teotihuacanos located north of México City.

Texas annexation   The annexation of the Republic of Texas by the United States; occurred after the Texas Revolution against México by Anglo Americans.

Tijerina, Reies López   Founder of La Alianza and leader of the land grant movement.

Tikal   A major pre-Columbian archeological site of the Maya civilization located in Guatemala.

Tolteca   A pre-Columbian civilization in central México at the city of Tula; known for their king, Quetzalcóatl.

Treaty of Guadalupe Hidalgo   A peace treaty between the United States and México as a result of the Mexican-American War, 1846–1848.

Treaty of Velasco   Treaty intended to conclude hostilities regarding the independence of Texas from México and signed by General Santa Anna.

Treviño, Jesús   Filmmaker. Jesús Salvador Treviño is a prolific television director.

Tulum   A major pre-Columbian archeological site of the Maya civilization located in the Yucatán Peninsula in the state of Quintana Roo.

Undocumented immigrants   Immigrants without U.S. legal documents for residency.

United Farm Workers of America   Labor union founded by César Chávez and Dolores Huerta.

Uxmal   A major pre-Columbian archeological site of the of the Maya civilization located in the state of Yucatán.

Valdez, Luis   The father of modern Chicano theater and one of the greatest dramatists of American history. Founder of El Teatro Campesino.

Vaquero   The Spanish word for cowboy.

Vásquez, Tiburcio   Known in California as a social bandit and legendary folk hero.

Victoria, Guadalupe   Fought for independence from Spain. The first president of México (1824–1829) following the fall of the empire led by Emperor Agustín de Iturbide (1822–1923).

Villa, Francisco "Pancho"   Mexican general during the Mexican Revolution of 1910; commanded the forces in northern México against President Porfirio Díaz.

Xenophobia, Xenophobic   A fear, distrust, or suspicion of people who appear strange, foreign, or different.

Zapata, Emiliano   Leading figure in the Mexican Revolution of 1910; commanded the revolutionary forces in southern México against President Porfirio Díaz.

Zoot suit; zoot suiters   Pachucos and pachucas during the 1940s who established a sub-culture and cultural style.

ABOUT THE AUTHOR

Arturo Amaro-Aguilar is professor of Chicano-Latino Studies at Fresno City College and a part-time lecturer in Chicano-Latin American Studies at California State University, Fresno. He is a graduate of Modesto High School, Modesto Junior College, and California State University, Stanislaus. Earning his M.A. from San José State University in Mexican American Graduate Studies, Professor Amaro-Aguilar has also done graduate coursework at the doctoral level. His research interests focus on the history, heritage and culture of Mexican Americans. He considers his highest honor and privilege as faculty sponsor of student organizations such as MEChA.

© Frank Bach, 2013. Used under license from Shutterstock, Inc.

Ernesto Che Guerava Monument and Mausoleum, Santa Clara, Cuba (near La Havana).

Note to Students About the Author. Based on my trip to Cuba, I want to share a few thoughts regarding Chicano-Latino Studies as it relates to Latino América. My experience as a Chicano in Cuba had a great impact on my perspective of Chicano Studies and higher education overall. Cuba has an extremely rich history, heritage and culture.

I had an opportunity to experience their cultural arts. This included music, dance, murals, and modern, folk and religious art. Their most impressive arts emanates from the spirit of the people in their communities.

Cuba's urban redevelopment project in *La Havana* is extremely impressive in terms of architecture and engineering. They are remodeling buildings hundreds of years old. Cuba is integrating a unique balance of art and science.

Cubanos are a proud people who have a strong belief in themselves and their society. They value their country but it is more than patriotism. They possess a strong spiritual strength and belief in their culture. In my personal opinion, Cuba's greatest strength is their youth. As an educator, I was proud to see and meet schoolchildren, happy and enthusiastic about life and learning.

I would like to express my sincere gratitude to the Cuban people for their hospitality and graciousness. From my perspective as a Chicano and in keeping with the philosophy of *Chicanismo,* I say: *Viva Che!*

Author pictured at Che Guerava Monument, Cuba.

Regarding early studies and research in Chicano Studies, Professor Soldatenko states about the author:

Arturo Amaro examined the impact of the capitalist culture on the Chicano(a) . . . . the psychological disorganization of the personality that capitalist culture causes to the individual.

—Professor Michael Soldatenko,
author of, *Chicano Studies, the Genesis of a Discipline.*